Nelion south-east side and Top Hut.

Kitchwa Tembo summit seen from the Col.

EAST AFRICA
International Mountain Guide

Kenya · Tanzania · Uganda · Zaïre
including Mount Kenya, Kilimanjaro and the Ruwenzori

Mountaineering, expedition climbs, rock climbs
trekking routes and cave exploration

ANDREW WIELOCHOWSKI

WEST COL PRODUCTIONS

East Africa International Mountain Guide

First published 1986 by
West Col Productions
Goring Reading Berks. RG8 9AA England

ISBN 0 906227 29 1

Printed and made in England by
Swindon Press Ltd Swindon Wilts.

All photographs, maps and diagrams by the author except half title and page 22 (Pamela Collomb) and page 108 (WCP Archives)

Note to reader. Due to an error in printing the photograph on the back cover of The Temple near Minto hut has been reproduced reversed left to right.

Contents

Illustrations

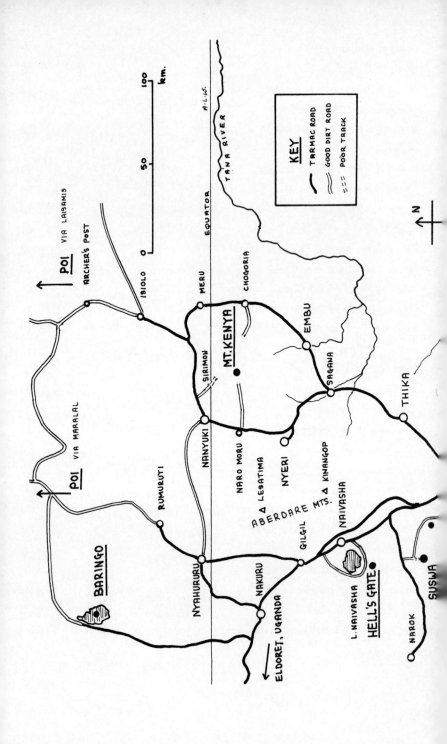

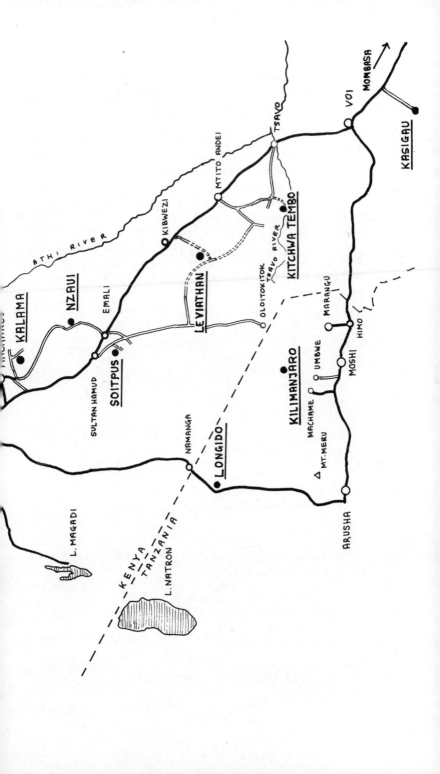

ACKNOWLEDGEMENTS

I have been gathering materials for this publication for nearly 8 years. The most enjoyable part of the work has been the actual climbing. Numerous people have offered a variety of advice and help. These include Peter Brettell, Simon Herd, Arshad Khan, Mark Kucharski, Dick Moss, Eliud Mwamburi, Olav Nilssen and Susan Swain. Ian Howell read most of the text and offered invaluable comments and information on routes and their descriptions. My wife Fay has had to endure endless requests for verification; her comments have been a great help, and I am also grateful for her support in pursuing the project.

Hillcrest Secondary School provided an Apple IIe computer. Without the help of the word processor and printer I would still be writing the guide. Ray Meynink, who runs the computer department, tolerated countless questions and allowed me to use his own computer and some drawing instruments for the maps and diagrams.

Ron Corkhill held the rope and enthusiastically climbed little known and obscure routes in order to judge their merit. He also did the bulk of the reading and correcting of the draft scripts. Many others have also been involved in the work; I thank all of them.

ABBREVIATIONS

biv.	bivouac (and site)
c.	circa (approx.)
gl.	glacier
h.	hour(s)
kg.	kilogram(s)
km.	kilometres
KSh	Kenyan Shillings (currency)
L	left (direction)
m.	metres
MCK	Mountain Club of Kenya
MCU	Mountain Club of Uganda
min.	minutes
R	right (direction)
R.	route number cross reference
TSh	Tanzanian Shillings (currency)
USh	Ugandan Shillings (currency)
YHA	Youth Hostels Association
YMCA	Young Mens Christian Association
YWCA	Young Womens Christian Association
Za	Zaire (currency unit)
4 WD	four wheel drive (vehicle)

N, S, E, W = north, south, east, west. Intermediate compass points, eg. NW (north-west), ESE (east-south-east), etc.

MAPS

All official mapping produced over East Africa in the British colonial period up to about 1970 is no longer in the public domain. Since independence the countries of East Africa, but notably Kenya, have kept a few key sheets in print and devised other types of large scale tourist mapping. However, the position in 1985 is that most of this mapping is out of print or withdrawn from public sale. Some of the maps may reappear in the future. Apart from national grid pattern cover in 1/50,000 over all areas in this guide, normally difficult to obtain, the following special sheets have circulated from time to time in the last decade.

> DOS = Directorate of Overseas Surveys (British)
> FNH = Forschungsunternehmen Nepal Himalaya
> SK = Survey of Kenya
> USD = Uganda Surveys Dept.

Kenya and Northern Tanzania 1/1,000,000 SK 81 2nd Ed. 1978. Includes all the ground from S of Kilimanjaro up to Mt. Kenya. Went out of print in 1985.

Mount Kenya National Park and Environs 1/125,000 DOS 2657 Ed.1. Produced by DOS for SK in 1974. Not available in 1985. A similar sheet over the Aberdare National Park was issued at the same time. Both reprinting for 1986.

Mount Kenya 1/25,000 SK 75 Ed. 5-SK. Inner park area. Originally DOS 302 flat sheet, reprinted in folded form by SK in 1973, and one subsequent printing. Not available in 1985.

Mount Kenya 1/5000 FNH, 1965. Good topo map of summit area, out of print. A half scale version in 1/10,000 was still available in 1985.

Kilimanjaro 1/100,000 DOS 522 Ed.1, 1965. Reprinted with colour variations including a version with trail routes, huts, etc. identified in red. Out of print (negotiations pending in 1985), copies have changed hands in the 1980s for £20.

Fort Portal 1/250,000 DOS base, issued by USD as Series Y503 Ed.1 in grid pattern series Sh. NA-36-9 in 1961. Only 3000 copies were printed. Covers the Ruwenzori and all approaches for some distance. Long out of print.

Central Ruwenzori 1/25,000 DOS base, issued by USD as a special sheet in 1970. Several printings exist, some in badly matched colours. Highly prized map, long out of print. A pilot version of same scale, constructed by photographic enlargement of 1/50,000 grid pattern sheets, dates back to the early 1960s.

A number of other special sheets over areas of less importance are excluded. Among these can be mentioned a park type map of Mt. Elgon in 1/125,000 (USD, 1967) and now rarely seen.

BIBLIOGRAPHY

Mountains of Kenya (P. Robson) EAPH/MCK Nairobi, 1969. Issued in hardback and stiff card cover, latter still available in 1986.

Guide to Mount Kenya and Kilimanjaro MCK Nairobi. Eds. 1-3 (1959-1971). Ed. 4 (I.J. Allan), 1982, out of print in 1986. Ed. 5 due in 1987.

Guide to the Ruwenzori (H.A. Osmaston, D. Pasteur) MCU Kampala / WCP Reading, 1972. Still available in 1986.

Rock Climbing Guide to the Main Wall and selected routes at Hell's Gate (I.J. Allan) MCK Nairobi, 1975.

Guide to Ndeiya (C.G. Powell) MCK Nairobi, 1968.

Outlying Crags (C.G. Powell) Nairobi, 1968.

A Climbers Guide to the crags of Lukenya (M.C. Watts) MCK Nairobi, 1973.

A Rock Climbers Guide to Kitchwa Tembo, Tsavo West Game Park (A.L. Wielochowski) MCK Nairobi, 1982.

A Climbers Guide to Embaribal (D. McMullan) MCK Nairobi, 1980.

MCK Bulletins, 1964 to date.

Cave Exploration Group of East Africa Bulletins, 1966 to date. CEGEA, PO Box 47583, Nairobi.

Kibo from the air, showing the southern glaciers.

Mt. Kenya south and south-west side from north flank of Teleki valley.

FOREWORD

IN February 1943 Benuzzi, Balletto and Barsotti escaped from a prisoner of war camp in Nanyuki with the sole aim of climbing Mount Kenya. They were inadequately equipped and their rations were meagre. The only route description they had was a picture of the mountain from a label on a tin of Kenylon minced beef. Under the circumstances they did well to reach the summit of Lenana and a point some 150m. below the summit of Batian on the West Ridge.

Since then route descriptions of climbs on Mt. Kenya and Kilimanjaro have progressed to the stage when today the 5th edition of a comprehensive guidebook to both mountains is in production.

But Kenya's climbing potential does not end with Mt. Kenya and Kilimanjaro. Due to East Africa's varied and active geological history the region has been left with an abundance of rock faces, towers and pinnacles. These are scattered from Tsavo in the north and range in height from a 5-metre boulder problem at Lukenya to serious big wall climbing on the 600m. flanks of Poi. East Africa must be one of the most exciting places for the keen rock climber, especially those who like exploring and are not averse to climbing in hot bush country.

This guidebook selects the best of these climbing areas and Andrew Wielochowski describes in a concise and factual way his personal recommended climbs on these crags and mountains. It will open up a new horizon of climbing possibilities, particularly for the visiting climber who will find this book an invaluable source of information for every kind of mountaineering objective.

Ian Howell

Mt. Kenya: Diamond Couloir headwall.

PREFACE

KILIMANJARO, first observed and recorded by Europeans in 1848, was the first major East African mountain to be climbed. After repeated attempts Hans Meyer and Ludwig Purtscheller reached the summit in 1889.

In 1887 the first large expedition approached Mt. Kenya, led by Count Teleki. It reached the higher moorlands. Subsequent expeditions explored more of the mountain. In 1899 Sir Halford Mackinder, Cesar Ollier and Joseph Brocherel climbed Batian. There followed a period of exploration of other routes; Eric Shipton climbed Nelion by the Normal Route and Batian by the West Ridge. Ernest Carr developed the Chogoria trail from the east to the mountain.

The Ruwenzori, protected by steep-sided, thickly vegetated valleys and perpetually shrouded in mists, repulsed several explorers. Eventually, in 1906, The Duke of Abruzzi reached the heart of the range, the Stanley Group. His expedition successfully tackled most of the major peaks for the first time.

By the 1930s there were a fair number of active climbers in East Africa and the Mountain Club of East Africa was established. Their first publication, The Ice Cap No.1, appeared in 1932, and in this all the important ascents to date were tabled. As more routes were climbed they were recorded in various journals and in the MCK Bulletins. In 1959 the first guidebook to Mt. Kenya and Kilimanjaro was published by the MCK, and in 1972 the MCU issued a guide to the Ruwenzori.

Lukenya, a fine area of outcrops near Nairobi, rapidly became a popular training ground. In Bulletin No.7 the first guide to Lukenya appeared. Subsequently two more guidebooks have been published, the most recent in 1973.

The development of harder routes on Mt. Kenya and of climbs on other crags in East Africa began in earnest in the 1960s with a spearhead led by Ian Howell and MCK members. The result of this activity produced guidebooks for a number of singular areas, including: Hell's Gate (Iain Allan and Phil Snyder), Outlying Crags (Colin Powell), Embaribal (Dave McMullan), Kitchwa Tembo (Andrew Wielochowski), Ndeiya (Reg Pillinger). Since their appearance many new routes have been put up and many new areas explored.

The purpose of this guide is to select the best routes from an enormous number now developed and disseminated in publications and circulars not generally available to the public. The caving section is intended to satisfy the numerous inquiries about this subject made by MCK members and visitors to Kenya. At present there is no readily available information elsewhere.

New routes, corrections and comments on this publication should be sent to the author at: Mountain Club of Kenya, PO Box 45741, Nairobi, Kenya, East Africa.

A.L. Wielochowski, January 1986

Hell's Gate : Andromeda.

INTRODUCTION

GEOGRAPHY AND PEOPLE

KENYA is a country of great beauty and variety. From the Indian Ocean it rises westwards in a series of steps. Beautiful beaches and fertile coastal plains give way to hot, semi-arid bush country renowned for its wild life. Cooler hilly zones in this hinterland receive more rainfall and are cultivated. On reaching Nairobi the plains stand at a height of 1500m. Further W the land rises again to give Kenya its luxuriant and fertile highland regions, cut by the spectacular, steep-sided Rift Valley, whose floor is hot and dry. Northern Kenya, thinly populated by nomads, is a semi-desert where water is scarce. Here the hills are lower and generally covered in forests and bush.

Many different tribes inhabit the country. The majority of the population around Nairobi belong to the Kikuyu tribe, an industrious pastoral people. Throughout Kenya the people are friendly, easy-going and are always willing to help visitors. However one must remember that the various tribes have different traditions and beliefs, and are proud of their own cultures. Many of them, such as the Masai and the Samburu, have not accepted Western values into their lives and continue living in what a European would consider a primitive manner. The nomadic tribes have a history of warfare and fighting and some of their belligerent characteristics persist. For instance, visitors have occasionally had spears thrown at them for being too snap-happy with cameras. Without prior permission or payment nomads believe that photography results in the theft of their spirit.

HISTORY

Kenya was created a modern state at the beginning of the 20th century when the British built a railway from Mombasa, through Nairobi, to Lake Victoria and Uganda. Initially it was administered by the British, but after agitation for independence culminating in the Mau-mau rebellion, the country was granted self-determination under the enigmatic figure of Jomo Kenyatta or "The Mzee" in 1963. Kenyatta was a well travelled man who had studied in many cities of the world and was imprisoned by the British during the Mau-mau period. He became the first President of the Republic and retained most of his European advisers and skilled personnel. Since then "Africanization" has taken place gradually, resulting in a stable, well-run democracy. When Jomo Kenyatta died in August 1978 the Presidency was taken over by His Excellency Daniel arap Moi.

ECONOMY AND CURRENCY

The country relies on exports of coffee, tea, sisal, cashew-nuts, etc. and tourism. While Kenya has suffered during the general recession, the economy has received a lot of support from external sources and remains buoyant compared to most African countries. Though most of the population is poor, free primary education is available to all Kenyan children; food is plentiful, medical facilities are adequate and the people are generally healthy, happy and proud of their country.

The Kenyan Shilling is not traded on the international monetary markets and can only be obtained in Kenya. It is the only legal currency and must not be exported. Monetary exchange regulations must also be adhered to strictly. In 1985, £1.00 sterling = 24 KSh.

Food prices, bus and train fares and basic accommodation are generally cheaper than in Europe or the USA. Imported goods and more exclusive services, such as 1st class hotels and taxis, are fairly expensive.

FOOD

Almost any food obtainable in Europe or the USA can be purchased in Nairobi, Mombasa and one or two other major centres. Dehydrated meals are not available but adequate alternative menus can be devised. Camping gas cylinders and paraffin are available. For petrol stoves, the so called "dry cleaning fluid" found in super markets is better than leaded petrol.

TRAVEL

Without your own transport travel can be tedious if you wish to reach more remote areas of the country. The most distant cliff can be reached in 12 h. driving from Nairobi. Rates for hiring vehicles tend to be high. A fairly competitive charge for a small saloon car is 3500 KSh for a week (unlimited mileage). Public transport is efficient. Most villages have a daily bus or matatu service; the latter is a very crowded van or car, renowned for high-speed, breathtaking travel. The majority of the areas in this guide are served by this transport, followed by a short trek to the climbs. Invariably having your own vehicle is more convenient. Train services are only useful on the Nairobi-Mombasa run, or for entering Uganda.

MOUNTAIN CLUB OF KENYA

The MCK meet at their clubhouse at Wilson Airport every Tuesday evening. It is often possible to arrange lifts among the members to various places. The club has an extensive library and map collection, sells guidebooks and is a useful source of information. A 6 months temporary membership costing 100 KSh can be advantageous for certain trips. Members are automatically entitled to the Flying Doctor service (free) which can be summonsed through any Police Station, hospital or major hotel, or by telephoning Nairobi 336886 or 501280. Address: MCK, PO Box 45741, Nairobi, Kenya. Tel: 501747.

RESCUE FACILITIES

A civilian rescue team is based in Nairobi. The MCK should be contacted if any technical assistance is required. On Mt. Kenya, the park rescue team will carry out straightforward rescues. Well managed rescues have been carried out in Kenya but visitors must remember that wherever they are climbing they are very much on their own; rescues from more remote areas and from harder routes on Mt. Kenya could take several days. See also Flying Doctor service mentioned in the previous paragraph.

HEALTH

Well equipped hospitals throughout Kenya provide good services, and treatment can be obtained at modest rates. Specialized treatment is best sought in Nairobi and private treatment (fairly expensive) would be advised if long waiting is to be avoided.

Numerous tropical diseases exist in East Africa but even the most endemic can be avoided by basic precautions. Kenya on the whole is disease free and the standards of health and hygiene are high. A few areas are malarial, notably the coast and Lake Victoria. Insects are not a nuisance and repellants need not be carried except occasionally in malarial areas. Walking through high grass in game or cattle country can result in ticks being picked up. These should be removed as soon as possible; though painless, they can cause a viral tick-fever which is difficult to cure.

FLORA AND FAUNA

A tremendous variety of plants and animals is encountered in this safariland par excellence. Generally, if given sufficient warning, wild animals and reptiles will retreat but make sure they have an escape route. When trapped even the most timid looking wild animal may attack. Also, never become caught between a big animal and her young. Hippo may attack if cut off from water, and exercise special care when near elephant or buffalo. While collecting firewood or lifting stones, look out for scorpions; their bite, though rarely deadly, is extremely painful. On climbing routes bees nests must be avoided. African bees are aggressive. They readily attack and a swarm can kill. Hornets will also be found occasionally on climbs. Often they can be climbed past or beaten off, but great care should be exercised as their stings are temporarily very painful.

SECURITY

Theft is not a serious problem but sensible precautions should be taken. When leaving a car or tent, take valuables away or conceal them in the boot of a car. Where possible leave a car or camp in the care of someone, eg. a guard (askari).

NAIROBI

The capital was born when the railway builders reached the cooler, lush highlands. Here they decided to base their administration centre to govern the land between Mombasa and Uganda. Nairobi is a Masai word meaning cool water. Modern Nairobi is a big European style city with all the associated amenities.

The airport is 15 km. from the town centre. Cheap Kenya Airways buses provide a regular service to most places in central Nairobi; taxis are expensive. The layout of the city and its environs are complex and a map of the town can be purchased at any bookseller. Though maps of Nairobi and road maps of Kenya are available, other maps are almost impossible to obtain; try making an official application to the Survey of Kenya offices.

Buses and matatus provide a cheap form of travel within Nairobi and a journey in the city should rarely cost more than 5 KSh. Travel beyond Nairobi is also cheap, eg. a matatu to Naro Moru costs about 100 KSh. An efficient bus service to most towns in Kenya is provided by the Rift Valley Peugeot (RVP) and the Mombasa Peugeot Service (MPS) among others. Information about matatus, RVP, MPS and Kenya Bus Service (KBS) can be obtained by making inquiries in the neighbourhood of Tom Mboya Street or by telephoning the appropriate company. Kenya Railways operate a useful and pleasant overnight service to Mombasa. There are numerous cheap hotels in central Nairobi, eg. along Tom Mboya Street. These are convenient for shopping and travel. There are mnay other convenient hotels and hostels; among the less expensive ones are:

Parkhill Hotel, Monrovia St, next to Jeevanjee Gdns. PO Box 32993. Central location. Tel. 333445.

Hotel County, Uhuru Highway/Haille Selassie Ave. PO Box 41924. Central location. Tel. 26190 or 337621.

Some East African animals: top left – young lion; centre left – rhino; bottom left – elephant; top right – zebra and wildebeest, giraffe inset; centre right – colobus monkey; bottom right – wildebeest and Thomson's gazelle.

YHA, Ralph Bunche Rd, PO Box 48661. Tel. 723012. 2 km. from town. Well run, has no food but kitchen facilities are available.

YMCA, Muhoho Ave, PO Box 59260. Tel. 556419. 2 km. from centre, near the "South C" shopping centre, Uhuru Highway and Wilson Airport.

YMCA, State House Rd, PO Box 63063. Tel. 337468. Near centre.

YWCA, Mamlaka Rd (near Serena Hotel), PO Box 40710. Tel. 338689 or 335794. Near centre. Cafeteria services available.

The suburban centres of Hurlingham and Westlands have excellent shopping facilities, 2 km. and 4 km. respectively from the city centre. Within the city there are several good supermarkets; the best is probably Uchumi on Muindi Mbingu St, close to the city market. Beware of petty theft in hostels and hotels.

LANGUAGES

Each tribe in Kenya has a different language. At school every Kenyan learns Swahili and English. As a result most Kenyans speak reasonable Swahili and some will speak English. Children often speak the best English. Below are some words from which a very ungrammatical but understandable Swahili could be spoken.

Nouns:

animal	mnyama	hour	saa	rain	mvua
banana	ndizi	hut	nyumba	river	mto
chief	jumbe	lamp, light	taa	salt	chumvi
danger	hatari	load	mizigo	saucepan	sufuria
day	siku	man, men	mtu, watu	sugar	sukari
European	mzungu	matches	kiberiti	snow, ice	barafu
evening	jioni	meat	nyama	tea	chai
fire, heat	moto	milk	maziwa	tent	hema
fish	samaki	minute	dakika	today	leo
flour-maize	posho	morning	asubuhi	tomorrow	kesho
flour-wheat	unga	night	usiku	water	maji
food	chakula	path, track	njia	week	wiki
hill	mlima	pay	mshahara	wood	kuni

Verbs:

bring	leta	eat	kula	see	ona
carry	beba	fasten, close	funga	sleep	lala
clean	safisha	give	kupa	undo	fungua
come	kuja	go	kwenda	wait	ngoja
cook	pika	know	jua	want	taka
do	fanya	say	sema		

Numbers:

1 moja, 2 mbili, 3 tatu, 4 nne, 5 tano, 6 sita, 7 saba, 8 nane, 9 tisa, 10 kumi, 11 kumi na moja, 20 ishirini, 30 thelathini, 40 arabaini, 50 hamsini, 100 mia, 1000 elfu, half = nusu.

Other words and phrases:

cold	baridi	good	mzuri	bad	mbaya	far	mbali	near	karibu
small	kidogo	big	mkubwa	ill	mgonjwa	up	juu	down	chini

23

quickly	upesi	slowly	pole pole	and, with	na	not, don't	hapana
yes, it is so	ndiyo	not yet, later	bado	for, to, at	kwa		
there is	iko	how many ?	ngapi ?	who ?	nani ?		
where ?	wapi ?	what ?	nini ?	why ?	kwa nini ?		
here	hapa	there	uko	how	namna gani		
very	sana	thus	namna hi	hello	jambo, habari		

habari means "how are you?" and requires a reply of "mzuri"

good bye	kwaheri	thank you	asante	I, me	mimi	us, we	sisi
you	wewe	he, him	yeye	they, them	wao	this	hi	now	sasa
all	yote	much, many	mingi	soon	bado kidogo		

Swahili time is based on 6 am or 6 pm being called 12 o'clock (saa kumi na mbili).
Eg. 7 am or 7 pm is saa moja. 1.30 is saa saba na nusu. To distinguish am and pm
use asubuhi (morning), usiku (evening).

Ndiyo means more "that is so" rather than yes.

Pronunciation is phonetic. All e's are as in "men", a's as in "banana", i's as in
"be", o's as in "go", u's as in "too".

CLIFFS AND CLIMBING IN EAST AFRICA

The style of climbing can be largely predicted by the area concerned. Rift Valley
crags in the western areas such as Hell's Gate, Ndeiya, Baringo and Embaribal are
composed of columnar lavas in which smooth walls and vertical cracks abound. At
Hell's Gate the commendite rock forms tall hexagonal columns divided by wide,
smooth-sided chimneys and cracks. Bands of rotten rock are occasionally encountered in these formations. The final pitch of Hell's Gate's hardest climb, Andromeda,
has been described as vertical cornflakes.

E of the Rift Valley, in northern Kenya, giant batholiths of gneiss or granite tower
above the semi-desert. Their summits and lower slopes are often covered in thickets,
and the rock walls are steep, smooth and featureless. Lack of freeze-thaw action
and heavy rainfalls as are experienced in Europe prevent the formation of extensive
cracks and erosion features. Instead exfoliation is more commonly found. Lack of
water, high temperatures when in the sun and dry air add to the problems of climbing on these cliffs. A spectacular example is the cliff at Poi. This batholith is 3 km.
long and encircled by cliffs which on 3 sides are never less than 300m. high. The
easiest route to the summit is grade III and involves a 2-day expedition.

Between Nairobi and Mombasa there are several good climbing areas, eg Lukenya
and Tsavo. The rock varies; in the two mentioned it is composed of a high-quality
gneiss. Schists are also found in this area, eg in the Taita Hills. Here the rocks
are generally more heavily cracked and eroded than those of northern Kenya.

Mt. Kenya is an ancient volcano. At one stage it was higher than Kilimanjaro
(probably over 7000m.). Throughout the millenia erosion has worn it down to its
present height. The lower slopes form a great circle of some 100 km. in diameter.
The slopes rise gradually from about 1500m. to the summit area which is the plug of
the volcano. Now it is heavily eroded and sculptured, mainly by glacial action, to
give the summits their present form. Numerous smaller peaks surround the 2 main
summits of Batian and Nelion. The phonolite rock is rough, hard, crystalline and
well fractured by frost, providing excellent climbing. Mt. Kenya also has some
excellent ice climbs; the Diamond couloir is probably the best known climb in East
Africa.

Climbing Point Dutton in the Mt. Kenya massif.

Kilimanjaro used to be in Kenya; for various political reasons it was given as a birthday present to Kaiser Wilhelm by Queen Victoria, so that the border between Kenya and Tanganyika was redrawn. In the recent past, friction between Kenya and Tanzania has made it difficult to cross the border but in 1983 it was reopened. So access to this magnificent mountain is now relatively straightforward from Kenya. Though the rock on "Kili" tends to be rotten, the precipitous SW slopes are heavily glaciated and these glaciers provide superb routes to the summit. Some brief notes about other areas from which climbs are selected:

(a) Lukenya, Ndeiya and Embaribal. Popular because of ease of access from Nairobi, their pleasant setting and good quality climbing.

(b) Hell's Gate, though further away in the Rift Valley, provides a variety of sensational longer climbs.

(c) Tsavo. Here the cliffs are located inside a game park. Access requires advanced planning but this is rewarded by the exotic situation and high quality climbs.

(d) Poi, Nzaui and Baringo. All have something unique to offer. Poi reveals Kenya's current biggest wall climb. Nzaui makes for a pleasant excursion. The short, varied climbs at Baringo are located on a small island, reached by swimming or boat from "Island Camp" - a beautiful, luxurious tented camp.

WEATHER AND CLIMATE

As a result of the high altitude and dryness, the air is cool and fresh over most of Kenya, though temperatures can become very high in the direct sun around noon. There are 2 rainy seasons; the "Long Rains" occur between the end of March and the middle of May; the "Short Rains" normally start in late October and finish in early December. During these periods the weather is more humid. Rainfall occurs most often as short, sharp showers in the afternoon, or in the highland regions as longer periods of overnight rain. Lying directly on the equator Mt. Kenya has sun on its S side between December and March. This time is best for S-facing rock climbs but not suitable for the ice climbs on this side. Between May and October the N-facing rock and the S-facing ice are in condition.

Kilimanjaro's cliffs are S-facing and ice climbs are at their best either in late December or very early January before too much thaw has occurred after the short rains; or in the cooler May to October period. In general for other cliffs the best seasons or times of day are when the sun is off the cliff. Thus S-facing cliffs are best in the May to October period, E-facing ones are best in the afternoon, etc.

CLIMBING HAZARDS

Most crags other than Lukenya and Hell's Gate could be described as bush crags. Their approaches are frequently through tangles of bushes, cactuses, thorn trees and vines. Chimneys and cracks sometimes harbour a ferocious cactus or some other exotic plant. Apart from bees and hornets (mentioned previously) bats also often live in the cracks. Being fruit bats they are not rabid. Many birds inhabit the crags - notably owls, eagles, vultures and other birds of prey. These are not a serious hazard. Snakes may be found on ledges. In 8 years of intensive climbing the author has not encountered a single snake on an African crag. Given enough warning of your approach they will generally slither away.

EQUIPMENT

No special equipment is needed, and pegs are rarely required; essential pegs are mentioned in descriptions. On Mt. Kenya pegs should only be used on ice climbs.

Embaribal: Amundsen's Original Route.

In Tsavo and the Rift Valley crags big chocks and "friends" are useful for wide fissures. A waterbottle should be taken on any long bush route because dehydration can be serious.

Climbing in shorts and a short sleeved shirt is normal, but long trousers and a tough shirt are often best for pushing through the bush; an alternative are shorts and a pair of canvas gaiters. On cliffs such as Hell's Gate or Nzauni cloudy days in July and August can be quite cold.

CHALK

So far all climbs in Kenya have been done without chalk and have been graded accordingly. It is hoped that climbers will not use chalk in the future, as this will save routes from being defaced and make chalkless climbing easier.

GRADINGS AND QUALITY RATINGS

Various grading systems have been experimented with in East Africa. In this work the UIAA is adopted for rock climbs, and the Scottish for snow/ice routes. For comparison with other systems:

English		UIAA	American	Scottish	French
Easy		I	2		F
Moderate		I+	3		F+
Difficult		II	4.0–4.4	1	PD
V. Difficult		III	4.5–4.9	2	AD
Severe		IV	5.0–5.3	3	D
Hard Severe	4a	IV+	5.4		D+
	4b	V–	5.5		TD–
Very Severe	4c	V	5.6	4	TD
	5a	V+	5.7		TD+
Hard V.S.		VI–/VI	5.8–5.9	5	ED–
E1	5b	VI+	5.10a		ED/ED
E2	5c	VII–	5.10b/c	6	XD–
E3	6a	VII	5.10d/5.11a		XD

Gradings generally do not reflect the degree of protection available or seriousness unless this is of particular relevance, in which case it is mentioned in the route description. Quality ratings do not take route length into account.

*** = Excellent   ** = Very good   * = Good   No star = of some interest

If a route is poor, this is stated.

POPULAR CLIFFS

Lukenya

General: One of the most frequented cliffs in Kenya, consisting of several outcrops with a max. height of 100m. and reached in a few min. from a car. Also popular with birdwatchers and picnickers. Facing E, the afternoon and early morning are the best times for climbing. Water is only obtainable from nearby farms; camping possible at the lower picnic tree, though the best site is on the summit. Athi River has a petrol station and garage (12 km.). Check security situation with MCK.

Access: 40 km. from Nairobi beside the Mombasa road. After passing the cliffs, on a downhill part of the road, take a wide dirt road L and follow this for 400m. to where a track (for pedestrians) crosses a bank towards the cliffs. The official access (cars) follows wide dirt road for 1.25 km. from the main road, to where a track turns L. Take this till a track leads sharp L; go along this to a turn-off R bearing for the cliffs and ending by the lower picnic tree.

For the summit campsite ignore the sharp L and continue to a farm; beyond, the track ascends, turns W and attains the ridge crest. Turn off L and go past a beacon to the top. Cars trying to reach the summit may be turned back at the farm if MCK membership cards are not produced.

EDINBURGH CASTLE

Impressive cliff seen on L skyline, easily reached from the summit or picnic tree.

1 The Keep VI+ 55m. ***

.F. Howell, I. Allan, B. Thomas, 1976. Start at R end of the slabby section, where cliff becomes vertical. Just R of this point the lower walls are obscured by trees.

A steep slab on widely spaced holds to a tiny ledge and belays (20m.). Slightly R, then climb to a hole and excellent runner; move L to 2 pegs in place. Now several hard moves up to a horizontal crack system (peg far R). Climb to a bolt (crux), step R then take shallow corner to easier ground (35m.); a magnificent, sustained and adequately protected pitch.

2 Princes Street VI+ 55m. **

.Allan, R. Higgins, 1968. A fine climb but poorly protected.

A bulging wall one m. R of the Keep. Climb bulge and smooth wall to crack, leading up to L side of big flake; belay (20m.). Above flake step L to horizontal crack. Go up delicately to bolt. Traverse R below overhangs to tiny resting ledge (crux). Move up crack to R end of L overhang, then easier above to top (35m.).

3 Committee Wall (by Golden Anniversary start) V+ 45m. **

At R end of main wall, just L of a vegetated gully. From top of a block step on to wall. Move several m. L across a holdless scoop to gain a juggy wall (poorly protected) and climb this to a keyhole belay (25m.). Go up and surmount a bulge (strenuous) to ramp. Move L to reach easier ground (20m.).

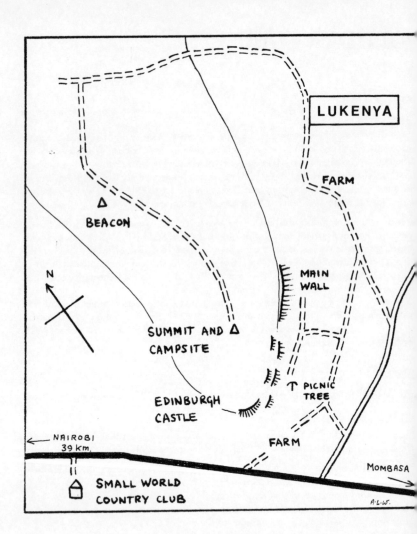

Committee Wall (V+ *) attains the keyhole by a long traverse from L. Golden Anniversary (VI- *) works R from the keyhole to surmount a bulge and gains the ramp further R, then a hard traverse L to rejoin the Wall finish.

EGYPTIAN CRAG

The lowest cliffs, some 150m. S of the picnic tree. At the R end a great fig tree obscures the chimney of Sphynx. A few m.L, a chimney-groove marks the start of Scarab. Further L a short vertical wall leads to a small terrace; above its L end a very steep, wide corner-with-crack is Papyrus. Bees may be encountered on the last 2 climbs.

4   Papyrus   IV+   25m. *

A.Owen, F.Richardson, 1961.

Start at a groove below L end of terrace. The groove and steep corner above to ledge; belay possible. Pull over bulge to easier ground above.

5   Scarab   IV   25m. *

W.M.Adams, 1961.

Climb into niche, step L and ascend directly to top.

6   Sphynx   V   20m. *

G.B.Cliff, R.Smith, 1960.

Climb the chimney and crack above to fault and roof. Over this on R to top.

Just L of Sphynx swing with difficulty onto the wall and climb more easily to top (Sweet Fanny Adams, V+).

ARCHWAY CRAG

R of Egyptian Crag and 50m. S of the picnic tree. A big fig tree in the centre of it marks the start of Tramlines. At the L end, just L of a gully-chimney, a fine, but unprotected slab gives Lichen (IV *). R of gully, at L end of grey slabs, the Original Route (I *) traverses R along a ledge towards a fig tree and climbs a grey slab direct. To the R the base of the cliff is shady. A groove line leading to holes in bulges marks the start of Standard Route. 3m. R, in an open area and above a tiny pigeon hole foothold, a wall leads to a small tree then a bulge on the R is climbed direct (Direct Route, III); an alternative start, several m. R, takes a R-facing corner to a bulge and crack above (IV). Subway (V+ *) starts 2m. R of R-facing corner and climbs a steep wall to a tiny spike, then 2 hard, fingery moves up a groove to easier ground.

7   Standard Route   III   35m. *

From the R-most tree in shady passage climb a groove and go over a bulge with holes to easy slab and the top.

8   Tramlines   IV   30m. *

Layback to top of the flake behind the central fig tree. Step L to ledge with a bush. Move R across steep wall and climb twin cracks to slab and top.

KEYHOLE

1 2 3

A·L·W·

9   Junction   VI   30m.

W.M.Adams, R.Searle, P.Le Pelley, 1960. Climb face of flake of R.8 to a
ledge. Climb to overhang and go over this (crux) to an easier slab.

The slabs just R of Junction are climbed by Boiler Plate (VI- *).

THE CEMETERY, EAGLE'S NEST FACE, FIG TREE WALL

An almost continuous wall starting above the L end of Archway and finishing above
Boulder. The last 2 sections are separated by a great fig tree, marking the base of
an easy descent route. The climbs are described from L to R.
   Above the highest rocks of Archway, note a L-facing corner and slab to L of it,
with a coffin-like stone at its foot; from this Tombstone (V *) climbs the slab some-
what R-wards. Just L, a groove leads to a short corner below an overhang which is
avoided on the L (Tidy, III+ *).

10   Cemetery Corner   IV   20m.   *

Start at the R side of this slab below the L-facing corner. Move up L below a
small overlap, then back R into corner. Climb to a small tree and ledge then
traverse L and up to a tree belay.

From the foot of R.10 a bushy ledge runs up and R to a platform with tree stump. A
steep crack above is climbed by Epitaph (VI). Just L is Cemetery Wall (V *); work
L then up to resting ledge; steep crack than slabs to top. The platform forms a R -
facing corner below. This leads to a long R-ward rising traverse (Eagle's Nest
Crack, V).

11   Exhibition Wall   VII   25m.   **

M.Savage, A.Wielochowski (after top-roping), 1981.

Start 3m.R of Eagle's Nest Crack. Climb wall over slight bulge to a root runner,
move up to niche (bolt), climb past a peg and pocket to a quartz band trending
L, then up a crack to top.

12   Anglepoise   VII-   30m.   **

R.Baillie, R.Pillinger, T.Phillips, 1964. A fine sustained climb initially done with
aid. 4m.R of R.11 an overlapping crack system splits the blank wall.

Climb 2m. then step R to crack. Follow this to a layback (crux) just before
reaching Eagle's Nest Crack. Continue direct to a ledge R of a fig tree (20m.),
then easily to top (10m.).

13   Savage Waltz   VII   20m.   *

J.Fantini, 1979. 10m.R of R.12 a block lies on the ground; start 3m.L of this.

Climb bulge to crack and move up to runner by a sapling. Swing R and layback
to niche. Above, a horizontal crack leads R to easier ground (as for R.14).

14   Pig's Ear   VI   35m.   *

R.Baillie, Winnings, 1964.

From the block climb up and R over bulge to ledges; undercuts above (old peg),
then a hard move leads to an overlap. Jam then layback strenuously R to easier

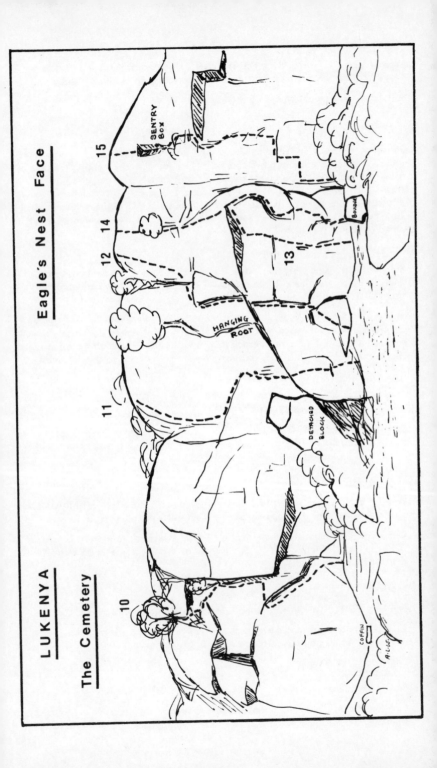

LUKENYA

Eagle's Nest Face

The Cemetery

ground (25m., tree belay). Easily to top in 10m.

15 Thin Wall Gable Finish   IV+   35m. *

Jenkins, Wilson, 1956. 2m. R of R.14 a root hangs to the ground.

Climb root then R on polished holds to a ledge (12m.). Turn the roof above on L (13m., tree belay). Climb the sentry box directly above, to the top.

16 Plunge   V–   25m. *

M.Harris, R.D.Metcalfe, 1967.

15m. L of large fig tree below the descent gully, climb a groove (initially hard) to overhangs and go through these L–wards.

R of the descent gully is Fig Tree Wall. 2m. L of the fig tree a groove marks the start of Turret Wall (III), turning the pear-shaped overhang on L, and finishing by a groove above. To the R are several pleasant routes (III–IV). Further R is a great long overhang.

17 Le Pelley's Variation   IV+   35m. *

Climb a R-facing corner (or wall just L) to a ledge under the roof. Belly crawl or hand traverse L to big ledge L of roof. Climb trending R (crux) to a ledge, tree belay (15m.). Walk 4m. R, climb cracks to easy ground and finish by chimney R.

The walls R of the roof are climbed by Cakewalk (III+ *); this starts at the centre of this area and climbs diagonally L-wards, passing a tiny tree, to finish by a specta-cular, exposed wall, above a roof and L of a second tree.

THE BOULDER AND JACOB'S LADDER

The closest outcrop to the R of the picnic tree, providing several short training climbs on excellent rock. Boulder 4 (II) climbs a groove in the centre. L of this Boulder 3 takes a steep wall (IV). To the R, Boulder 5 (IV–) gives a fine steep pro-blem. Just R of the Boulder, but L of a bay with overhangs, a slab–with–hole rises to a steep wall; above step R to above roofs (Bee Buttress, IV–). Further R the base of the cliff is obscured by trees and bushes. R of these is an open patch.

18 Jacob's Ladder   II   35m. **

An excellent beginners route. Climb a grey slab above the open patch, first to R via pigeon holes, then direct, passing a bulge near top on the L.

MAIN WALL

The biggest cliff, R of the access track. The L half has a long overhang at half height. The R end is easier-angled. The climbs are about 3 pitches long. Route finding is difficult and good protection is lacking, making the climbing serious.

19 Bandstand   V   70m. ***

W.M.Adams, Vandepeer, A.Owen, 1958. A great fig tree stands at the foot of the Main Wall. Start 10m. L of this, near the L end of a slab.

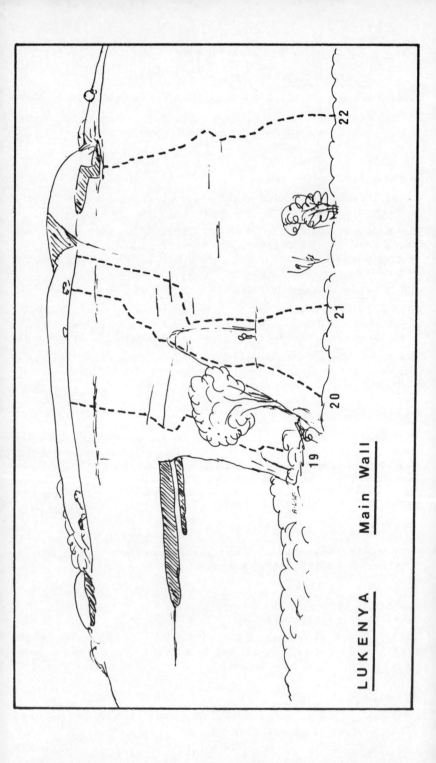

LUKENYA   Main Wall

Climb a steep slab then a crack and wall to ledge with 3 small trees (25m.); belay at L-most fig tree. Climb a white, pillar-like buttress behind tree, to move up and L of small nettle trees to a ledge overlooking the R-hand end of the long overhang (possible belay). Climb wall above the trees to horizontal crack and excellent runners, then go straight up and slightly L to a deep, wide crack (25m.). Step R and climb direct to the top (20m.).

20 Arthur's Horror IV 90m. ***

A.Firmin, Lord Howick. Start in the middle base of a black slab, below the great fig tree, at L end of the main sweep of slabs.

Climb slab to steep wall and up to platform (35m.). Now an easy buttress to a big ledge and blocks below the final, steepening wall (20m.). Follow slabs trending R to the headwall; move R to base of a narrow, cracked pillar. Climb this and a steep wall above to the top (35m.).

21 Colin's Caper IV- 80m. *

15m. R of Arthur's Horror and 10m. L of a "gully" with 2 nettle trees low down in it, climb a slab to grassy ledge with crack on L (20m.). Climb the slab just R of the flake-crack to big ledges (top of pitch 2, R.20) (30m.). Traverse R, keeping low below a bulge; then go directly up slabs and steep headwall to top (30m.).

22 Snake III+ 90m. ***

40m. R of the great fig tree another fig tree grows at base of the cliff with a corner behind it; 20m. R of this an upright, detached flake stands beside a small tree, and above this a crack with a recess L of it, 3m. off the ground.

Climb crack for 6m., step L and take slab to grassy bay (20m.). The next belay is directly above on a grassy ledge below a bulge (20m.). Move 2m. R to avoid bulge, then climb L-wards (long reach) to gain the higher of 2 recessed cracks above; an easier variant traverses further R from the belay to climb a cobblestone wall then move L to belay (20m.). Now go up direct to the top (30m.). Numerous variations L and R of Snake exist, all at about the same grade.

Above and slightly L of Main Wall, a huge boulder is split in two by a wide crack. This is climbed, some 7m. inside, and by facing L, by Wide Chimney (IV+ *); here are numerous caves and passages to explore.

Driving towards the picnic tree, the track makes a sharp L turn and becomes level. Almost directly above this point, and very near the top of the Lukenya ridge, is a big, pale brown cliff. At its L end, note a chimney with a red overhanging wall to its L. Further L is a grassy gully then a small, compact grey buttress. The L side of the big cliff has a huge flake crack running most of the way to the top, giving the line of Lizard, a Lukenya classic.

23 Lizard V+ 50m. ***

R.Baillie, R.Pillinger, 1964. Gain a tree at base of the flake crack, either directly up a vicious jamming crack, or further R by a blank groove, a slab, then traverse L (10m.). Step up and R to reach the crack; layback or jam up it to easier rock (40m.).

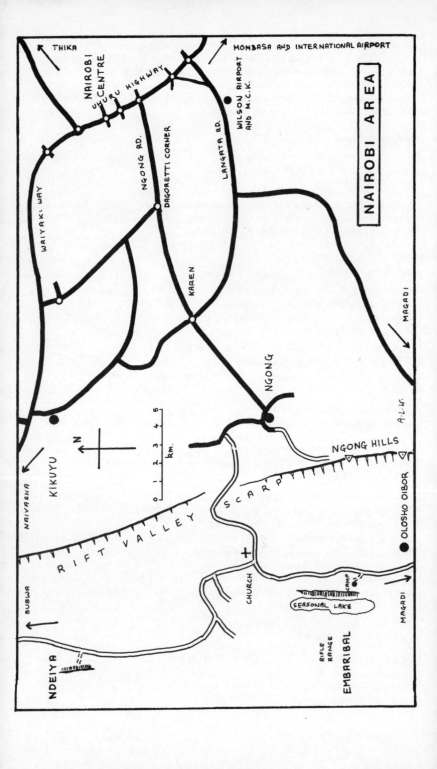

Embaribal

General: 30 km. from Nairobi, these cliffs are nearly 45m. high, extend for 4 km. and overlook a seasonal lake. Facing W, they can become unbearably hot on clear afternoons, though shady corners or chimneys can be found. The rock is a vertically cracked lava and the cracks sometimes house birds, bats, hornets and bees. The area is rich in bird and animal life. A variety of plants grow at the base of the cliff; beware of stinging nettles, pricking sansaferia (a type of cactus), and itching hibiscus – a tall plant covered with golden hairs. Masai use the area to graze cattle; they are friendly and often come up to watch climbers.

Locating routes is difficult because the access track is above the cliff. Descriptions are given in terms of metres N or S of an easily located feature. For first time visitors Le Pelley's Descent path is easiest to locate; it starts 30m. W of the first campsite (see below). At the bottom of the descent path walk either N or S alongside seasonal lake from where features on the cliffs can be more readily identified. There is no water near Embaribal; petrol station/garage in Ngong town (16 km.).

Access: From Nairobi follow the Ngong road as far as Ngong town. At a T junction in the town turn R and after 50m. R again at a traffic island. After 2.5 km. on tarmac, a good dirt road bears L and leads to the Rift Valley escarpment edge (fine viewpoint) then drops into the Rift Valley; after several km. a signposted junction beside a small church is reached.   Continue straight on and after 2.5 km. the road rises and winds slightly before a long level straight section is reached; 1.5 km. from the rise a big acacia bush and drainage ditch on the R mark the start of the access track (matatus from Ngong Town to Ol Oshoibor village pass this point).   Turn R over ditch and its bank then follow a track for 400m. to a sharp turn R by the first campsite. 700m. further N along a faint track reach a more pleasant campsite 150m. from the cliff edge. There are well over 200 climbs and only the best areas are described (from S to N).

FRENCH BUTTRESS

400m. S of Le Pelley's Descent, this impressive buttress has a grey wall to its L and a pale recessed area in the centre which tapers to a huge chimney blocked with large chockstones. R.24,25 are located either side of this pale area and both have very distinct starts.

24 L'Aiguille Perdue   V-   50m. **

A. Wielochowski, A. Haynes, M. Turner, 1979.   R of the prominent white walls of French Buttress, trees obscure the lower part of the cliff and a unique rock needle; approach from the R.

Climb a crack directly below the needle to ledge (10m.). Move L to the base of needle and climb it. From the top step onto a slab and move R and up (crux) to a crack slanting L. Climb this to a tree (20m.). Walk along tree branch to gain a slab above and take R edge of this to the top (20m.).

25 Pongo   IV-   50m. **

I. Allan, D. McMullan, 1979. Walking along base of cliff either from Le Pelley's Descent or from the bottom of an abseil down Alien (qv), 70m. S of latter, reach

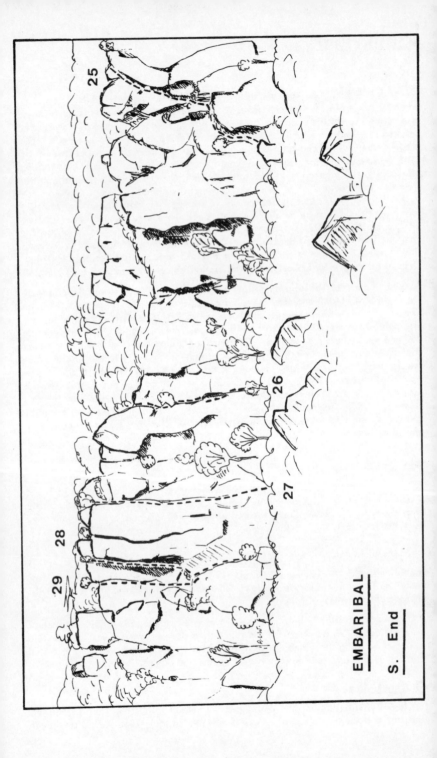

EMBARIBAL

S. End

the start just L of the pale walls on French Buttress where a huge block leans against the cliff, forming a tunnel. Gain the top of this block.

Move R to the base of a L-facing corner and climb this, stepping R below a tree, to a large terrace (25m.). Walk R over blocks, past a vegetated gully, to an easy-angled, R-sloping clean chimney. Climb this to the top (25m.).

Bastille (VI *) takes corners and walls L of the recessed area of French Buttress and finishes just R of Pongo. Last Tangle in Paris (VI- *) shares its start with Pongo but climbs a jamming crack above the L end of the block, then a squeeze chimney behind a detached flake and finally moves L, up a crack, turning a roof on the L.

SECOND AMPHITHEATRE

Reached by walking 250m. S from the bottom of Le Pelley's Descent; or better, but more difficult to find, walk 300m. S from the first campsite and beyond a wide depression turn W towards the cliffs. R of rock pinnacles (cairn) a low tree is used to make a long abseil down Alien to the bottom. Halfway down the abseil a vegetated bay is passed; this is the Second Amphitheatre. The routes leading out of this are good, but access from below (by Panga or Alien) is less pleasant.

10m. S of the bottom of the abseil is the start of Multiple Entry (R.27). 2m. L of this is the start of E.T. (VII **), a very hard route which climbs the buttress nose till a traverse L has to be made to enter an easy chimney.

26 Rapier V+ 45m. *

I.Allan, D.McMullan, 1979. S of R.27 the path drops round a rock nose and then becomes a narrow shady passage; at the end of this, 20m. from R.27, a single root comes down from a tree.

Climb to tree then a steep fingery crack above to an easier section and tree (25m.). Take the corner above, swing L and mantelshelf onto a slab. Move back R and climb awkwardly to the top (20m.).

27 Multiple Entry VI+ 40m. ***

P.O'Sullivan, R.Corkhill, 1981. A superb, hard and sustained route.

Climb a flaky slab and gain with difficulty the R-hand of 2 grooves. Layback up strenuously till a thin move L and up (crux) leads to a resting place. Above, an awkward move leads to the bottom of a chimney; climb this more easily to the top.

28 Panga V- 50m. **

A.Park-Ross, R.Chambers, D.Rudovitz, 1963.

Climb the R-most chimney into the amphitheatre (20m.). Scramble to foot of chimney on R wall of bay (10m.). Climb chimney, initially on L wall, near the top on R wall (20m.) - an excellent pitch always in the shade.

29 Alien VI+ 45m. *

I.Allan, V.Fayad, 1979.

Climb an unpleasant chimney with tree, L of R.28. Scramble to foot of a R-facing corner in centre of the bay (25m.); this pitch is best avoided. Climb

EMBARIBAL Bat Buttress

corner to a big ledge on L. Step R and climb steep wall to gain base of final R-facing corner. Go up this to the abseil tree (20m.); a fine, well-protected pitch with crux at top.

L of Alien a bottleneck chimney blocked at 3m. with a chockstone is climbed by B-Team (V+ *); the overhang near the top is taken direct.

40m. N of this area lies the 1st Amphitheatre. To its R is a high unbroken section of vertical rock bounded on the R by an off-width crack leading to a corner with a narrow chimney above (Thin Man's Start, IV+ *). To the R, in the Amphitheatre proper, there are several good routes: the R-most line is a thin crack gently trending R and ending in a short vicious corner above a platform; this is The Entertainer (VI *), starting in an overhung niche directly below the thin crack. Some 5m. L, Endangered Species (VI+ *) takes a gently overhanging jamming crack, reached up stepped ledges. 5m. further L a wide watershoot gives the line called Waterfall Chimney (V- *).

LE PELLEY'S DESCENT AREA

Walking S-wards from the bottom of the descent path a small buttress is passed. Beyond the path rises sharply. As it rises, on the L note a deep, diagonal chimney with the remains of a tree in it.

30   Piece of Cake   IV   40m. *

D.McMullan, F.Ellyatt, 1980. Pleasant but not well protected.

Climb the chimney and at the top traverse L to belay below a steep wall (10m.). The wall, moving slightly L at the finish, then straight up on big holds. A small bulge at 15m. is passed on the R, then easier to the top (30m.).

CENTRAL CLIFFS

N of the descent path the cliffs are relatively low for 300m., then they become broken; easy path to top here. 500m. N of Le Pelley's Descent a high section forms Bat Buttress. 200m. N again, a deep S-facing chimney, clearly visible from S, gives the line of Deep Throat (VI- *), a hard off-width crack. 20m. to L, the high cliffs contain a bay with 2 great corners facing each other (R end of Scoop Buttress); the R one is climbed by Bat out of Hell, a hard crack climb with a spectacular finish; the L one by Undertaker (VI+ *), a cleaner and less vicious route. To the L, Scoop Buttress provides several more fine routes; 2 good abseil trees serve the area (see diagram); these are directly W of the second campsite.

At 900m. from Le Pelley's Descent, the grey South Pole Buttress juts out from the cliff line; halfway up it is obscured by a big fig tree. It provides some fine climbing in a variety of grades. There is a good abseil tree just L of and below the top rocks.

A big fig tree grows at the foot of the R half of Bat Buttress. A corner facing R above is climbed by Ciborium Crack (VI- *); an overhang low down is turned on R and above a traverse L leads to a steep corner and the top. Enigma starts 6m. R of this, below a huge ear-shaped flake facing L.

31   Enigma   VI   47m. **

A.Wielochowski, D.McMullan, 1979. A fine climb.

Climb a groove to a roof (good runner), traverse L below this and climb a thin wall (crux) to reach good jams. Layback onto a small ledge. Continue up a

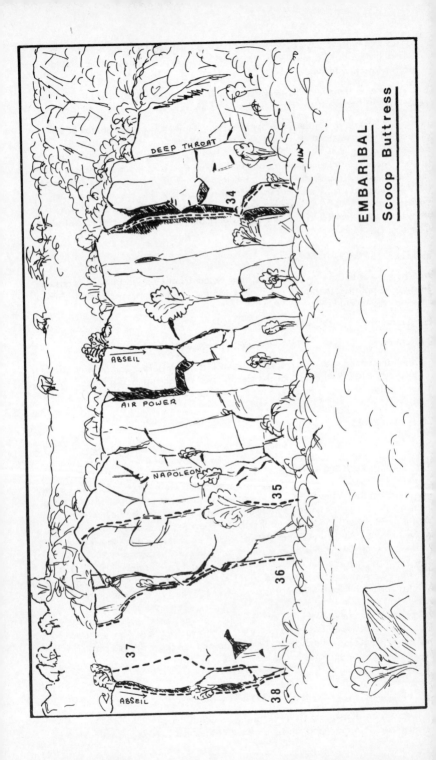

EMBARIBAL
Scoop Buttress

boulder filled chimney to the highest boulder (17m.). Step down and climb L across a steep wall, then up a slab (15m.). Climb a corner for 5m. Move R onto exposed wall and climb this trending R to top of buttress (15m.).

32 Psycho   VI+   45m. *

A.Wielochowski, I.F.Howell, 1979. 5m. L of fig tree climb a steep, cracked wall to a ramp trending R. Take this to a niche below a roof. Climb past roof on R (crux) to the top.

The Cauldron (VI-) starts 3m. L of R.32 at a L-facing corner; above this move R to base of the Psycho ramp but climb directly to a big ledge then up a corner on the L.

33 Desolation Crack   VI+   45m. *

A.Wielochowski, D.McMullan, 1979. The tall L half of Bat Buttress has a fierce crack splitting it - initially trending L and dirty.

Climb the chimney facing R and surmount bulge at the top (crux) to reach a resting place. The overhang above is turned by the L wall to a niche (25m.). Climb the crack to the top (20m.).

Further L the ground becomes more broken and vegetated. The hidden Catacoomb Chimney (II) leads pleasantly to the top. 100m. N of R.33 is Deep Throat; then L of this is Scoop Buttress which extends for 100m. and provides the next 3 routes.

34 Bat out of Hell   VI+   55m. **

M.Savage, A.Wielochowski, 1980. A dirty groove leads into the bay with the 2 great facing corners. 5m. R of this groove, a clean corner provides more pleasant access to the bay.
Climb the corner past a tree, traverse L with difficulty, then walk to base of the R-hand corner (20m.). Climb this to a cave; crux a few m. below cave (20m.). Take the overhanging chimney/crack system above till a move R leads to easy ground (15m.). The last pitch is improbable and spectacular.

Undertaker (VI+ *) shares the same entry pitch as R.34, then climbs the corner facing R above the bay. A flaring peapod near the top is avoided by moving L. 40m. N is another great L-facing corner in the upper half of the cliff. Air Power (V *) climbs this with fine hand-jamming; approach by corners and ledges from below and L. 10m. L of Air Power a short corner leads to a big ledge. Above are two crack systems; the R one has a dead tree in it halfway up, the L one, taken by Napoleon (VI *), is cleaner but peters out; at the top a small cave is quitted direct.

35 Uisge Beatha   V+   55m. **

A.Wielochowski, D.McMullan, 1979. Fine, hard jamming. 10m. L of the Napoleon access corner an obvious tree, 10m. up the cliff, has white roots coming down to the ground.

Climb to and past the tree to ledge (20m.). Move L into groove with 2 bulging cracks. Climb the R one then transfer to the L; continue past 2 ledges to a terrace (25m.). Climb an easy off-width crack on the L (10m.).

Aqua Vita (V+) climbs a crack system to the R of pitch 2 of R.35.

36 Changaa   V-   45m. *

A.Wielochowski, D.McMullan, 1979. Start 10m. L of the R.35 white tree root.

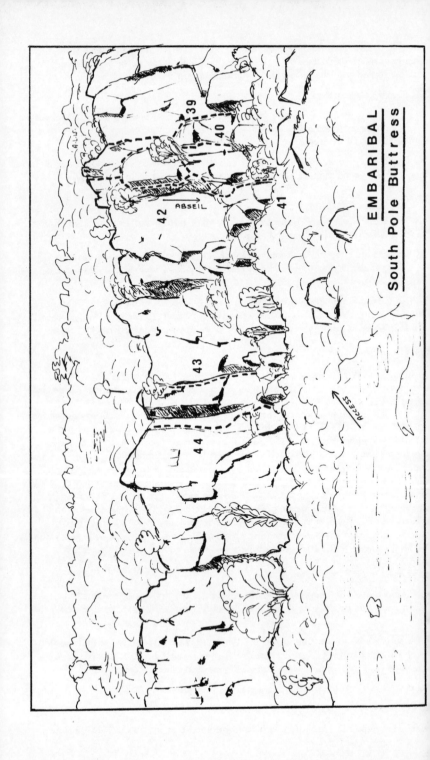

EMBARIBAL

South Pole Buttress

Climb a crack system to a ledge (15m.). Gain a chimney and above a chock-stone climb a crack on the L wall past a tree to a ledge (20m.). Move L onto a steep nose, climb this and wall above on small holds (crux) to the top.

20m. L of Changaa the tall buttress is bounded on its L by a great L-facing corner, with a small fig tree at half height. This is taken by R.38.

37 The Shield VII 40m. ***

A.Wielochowski (after top rope inspection), 1985.

The overhanging crack system just R of R.38. An obvious shield is the crux and is climbed by laybacking up its L side. Above, continue steeply to easier ground (possible belay). Follow crack to the top.

38 Bloody Mary VI+ 45m. **

A.Wielochowski, I.F.Howell, C.Dufourmantel, 1984.

Start at base of crag and climb a crack (IV+) to ledges below corner proper(10m.). Now the corner (VI-) to a tree (15m.). Continue (face L) over a bulge (VI+) and up a smooth corner (20m.).

The next 4 climbs are located on South Pole Buttress.

39 Where Eagles Dare VI- 50m. *

M.Savage, A.Wielochowski, 1980. R of the prow of South Pole Buttress there is a system of R-facing corners. To the R the walls overhang repulsively; below the L end of these is a giant detached block which forms a chimney leading to a plat-form.

Climb a steep corner 3m. L of chimney, till a mantelshelf move leads into a narrow chimney. Follow this (helmets off) to a long narrow ledge; bold leaders or large seconds could climb the outside of the chimney (20m.). This pitch can be avoided by climbing a pleasant pitch just R of R.40. Move to L end of the ledge and climb a bulging flaky crack to a cave (15m.). Take the crack above, awkward at first, to a tree and finish by moving L up a steep wall (15m.).

40 Footless Crow V 65m. **

I.F.Howell, A.Stephenson, 1979. Start 5m. R of a large fig tree growing out of the buttress at one third height.

Move up and L on ledges, then follow a good jamming crack to a small tree and a square cut roof. Layback past this on the L, using hand jams; climb to top of slab (25m.), at 1st belay of R.39. Move down and traverse L across a thin, steep wall to a tree at base of a crack. Climb this to a belay (15m.). Now a wide crack to a ledge below a slab. The slab and a steep corner above to the top (25m.).

41 Amundsen's Original Route V- 65m. ***

V.Fayad, A.Wielochowski, 1979. A pleasant varied climb.

From lowest point of the buttress climb 3m. to a ledge below an obvious peapod chimney; climb this to terrace (10m.). Walk 3m. R then follow a crack and slabs on L to a ledge below the main corner (10m.). From here go up and R diagonally, round a rib, to a ledge below overhangs. Traverse R, mantelshelf up, then move R to tree (15m.). The chimney behind tree to a ledge and from here as for pitch 3 of R.40. The main corner above pitch 2 is taken by Scott's Last Expedition (VI- *); the first few m. are climbed by the R crack; at the top of this corner is the abseil tree.

42 Grey Sérac V+ 35m. ***

A.Wielochowski, D.McMullan, 1979. One of the best pitches at Embaribal, it climbs the R wall of the Scott's Last Expedition corner. Almost always found in the shade. Start at top of pitch 2 of R.41.

Climb diagonally R past the rib, then go up to L end of a roof. Move L and climb past a tree to top of a grey flake. Follow the crack above to a ledge, then an easy slab and short corner to the top (35m.).

50m. L of the big tree on R.41 a higher terrace can be reached by a short scramble. At the R end of this terrace, and just R of a detached pinnacle, are twin cracks to the top, taken direct by Tropic of Capricorn (VI- *).

43 Equator VII- 25m. **

P.O'Sullivan, R.Corkhill, 1981. L of the pinnacle, a clearly visible and elegant crack line.
Climb crack to the top with the crux at 8m. Medium size Friends are useful.

44 Tropic of Cancer V 37m. *

V.Fayad, C.Swain, A.Wielochowski, 1979. 10m. L of the pinnacle, a bay with 2 corners facing each other. Start at foot of crag below this bay.

Climb a chimney in the corner; belay below the N-facing, R-hand corner (12m.). Traverse L up a ramp into the S-facing corner and climb this to the top; an elegant pitch (25m.).

Embaribal: The Shield.

Embaribal: Multiple Entry.

Hell's Gate: Milky Way and entrance to gorge below.

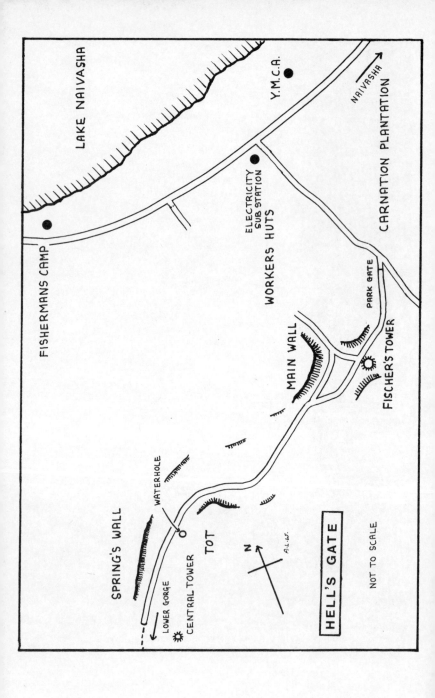

LAKE NAIVASHA

FISHERMANS CAMP

Y.M.C.A.

NAIVASHA

CARNATION PLANTATION

ELECTRICITY
SUB STATION

WORKERS HUTS

PARK GATE

MAIN WALL

FISCHER'S TOWER

WATERHOLE

SPRING'S WALL

TOT

CENTRAL TOWER

LOWER GORGE

N

A.L.W.

HELL'S GATE

NOT TO SCALE

Hell's Gate

General: Thought to have been formed by a river spilling out of Lake Naivasha in the past, this magnificent gorge with sheer cliffs rising to 150m. and renowned for its wildlife has recently been designated a National Park. The cliffs have deservedly become famous for their hard and serious climbing. The rock is composed of lavas cracked vertically to give columnar sections; sandwiched between them are narrow rotten bands. A band caps the central part of the Main Wall, giving Andromeda its horrific top pitch. Olympian, the first route climbed in this area, finds a way through the top rotten band by way of a safe chimney behind a huge hanging flake. Routes at the L end of Main Wall are mainly free of rotten rock.

All climbs can be reached in 5 min. from a car. Fischer's Tower, a small pinnacle at the entrance to the gorge, provides a variety of fine short climbs on good rock. As a Sanctuary, special care must be taken not to disturb nesting birds; this rarely poses any problems. The main cliffs face E, so climbing in the morning is not recommended unless the day is cool; climbing on Fischer's Tower, or exploring the lower section of the gorge, would be a pleasant alternative. Pegs are generally not needed. A wide selection of chocks should be carried, including a few of the larger hexentrics or Friends. Protection is generally excellent except in the rotten bands.

Camping is permitted in Hell's Gate but the final policy of the park authorities is at present undecided. An alternative campsite is at the YMCA, 2 km. away from the cliffs. Facilities here include cheap bands with beds and mattresses, a kitchen and showers. Similar amenities are found at Fisherman's Camp which lies some 2 km. beyond the YMCA on the main lake road. 7 km. away, towards Naivasha town, is Safariland Lodge; this offers more luxurious accommodation, good food, a swimming pool, beautiful grounds renowned for their birdlife and access to the lake. Petrol/garage at Naivasha town (15 km.).

Access: Good bus and matatu service Nairobi-Naivasha (1½ h.). Matatus and many other vehicles go down the South Lake Road which starts 2 km. S of Naivasha town. After 10 km. Safariland Lodge is passed on the R. In another 4.7 km., beside an electrical sub-station, lies the turn-off for Hell's Gate. The Park Gate and entrance to the gorge are 1.5 km. along this track. Fischer's Tower and the Main Wall are a few hundred m. into the gorge.

FISCHER'S TOWER

This obvious 50m. pinnacle offers shady climbing at any time of day. Descent is by abseil from an awkwardly placed ring bolt. Climbs are described from the E, anticlockwise.

45 <u>Original Route</u> IV+ 40m. *

H.C.Pereira, J.Moore, 1949. At SE foot of tower gain a cracked, easy-angled ridge by pulling over a steep nose. Trend L to a large fig tree, belay possible. Move up into a steep clean corner and take this direct, or more easily after 2m. move R round arête and climb to ledges above. From R end of these either go up steep cracks direct, or spiral up ledges to top. Var: from the easy ridge, traverse 2m. R to a slab and overhanging corner. Bridge over this to gain a slab on R. Traverse R below a small tree and climb a corner to reach ledge below the summit block. Then as above (IV−).

46 The Groove   V+   40m. **

M.Harris, I.Howell, 1967. The most obvious, roof-capped corner overlooking the picnic lawn on N side of tower. Climb groove in its entirety, moving L at the overhang.

47 Recompense   V−   45m. **

M.Harris, C.Powell, D.Metcalfe, 1966. Climb a few m. up The Groove till it is possible to traverse R to ledge above a tree. Move up R and climb across an arête (crux); pull R, round next arête. Turn roof on R and climb cracks to top.

Just L of The Groove an interesting route, The Bulge (VI− *), follows a crack to top of a pillar. Pull over the bulge (crux) into a niche; exit on the R by a strenuous crack. Compensation (V+ *) starts 4m. R of The Groove, at a steep black wall. Climb a L-trending groove above, swing R to a slab and ledge; then a crack system above goes to the top.

48 East Rib   IV+   40m. *

I.Allan, P.Sutcliffe, 1966. A steep rib facing oddly almost S. Walls and ledges lead to the rib which is climbed direct to the top.

MAIN WALL

This lies just beyond Fischer's Tower, on W side of the gorge. Climbs are described from L to R. 200m. from the L end is the Left End wall. 20m. above the ground a small green tree grows out of the cliff with its white roots trailing to the ground. This is one of the few unique features of this section. 5m. L of a point directly below the tree is the start of Magician. 12m. L of tree, 2 great boulders lie right beside the cliff; just L is the var. start to Merlin; 15m. above is the long corner pitch, capped by a roof. The original start is 20m. L of the tree, below a 10m. flat topped pillar, and 2m. R of FS scratched on the rock. 15m. further L, an unusual, horizontally striated and pocketed wall is seen, the start of Future Shock. Again 15m. further L, a big pale corner halfway up the cliff; this is taken by the Great Corner (VI+ *), a hard route starting some 10m. further L, up shattered columns just R of a fresh rockfall; 5m. above a line of roofs a long traverse R is made (V+) to a belay on the L arête, below the corner proper; the corner is entered over a hard bulge; near its top a swing L (VI+) leads to a belay from which a spectacular, and improbable traverse across the R wall (VI+ at end) leads to easier ground. The Left End climbs are all excellent and the rock is good where it matters.

49 Future Shock   VI+   110m. **

A combination of 3 old routes: Future Shock, Juggernaut, First Aid. All required aid on their first ascents. As described, the easiest and probably the most pleasant way up this area of rock; no aid is required.

Climb wall on pockets then easy R-trending cracks till a difficult move leads to roofs, 20m. up. Swing R on good holds below the roof to gain a groove, and continue R to a wide crack. Pull over a bulge above this, then climb a L-facing corner to a ledge (35m.). Continue to a niche, above and slightly R, then a steep corner with purple rock; a fierce layback leads to the easier corner above. A bulge in this is avoided by more broken ground on R. Move L to top of corner, then climb rotten rock L to a good belay below a steep corner, clearly seen from

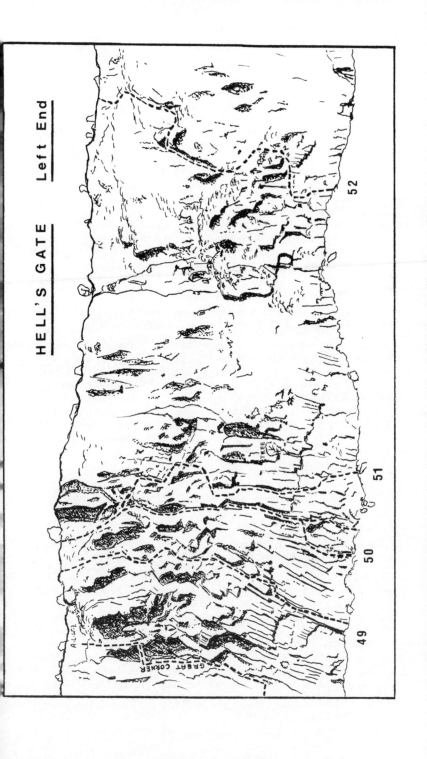

HELL'S GATE   Left End

the road (35m.). Pull into corner awkwardly; after 3m. traverse R and climb good rock till the angle eases; the more rotten rock above is climbed bearing L.

50 Merlin VI+ 100m. ***

I.Howell, I.Allan, 1977. A superb, sustained and well protected route, probably the best at Hell's Gate.

Climb a pillar and blocks, then a R-leaning, widening crack to a ledge R of the flat-topped pillar. A 3m. long grassy traverse R leads to the bottom of a long corner-groove system, terminating in a roof 40m. above the ground. Climb this over bulge (VI-) to small ledge on the L (30m.). Var: slightly harder but better. From just L of the 2 boulders climb to block on pedestal at 5m., then move R past a roof (VI) to bottom of the long corner; above rejoin the original line. Climb a thin crack R of ledge (VI) to roof, and from a peg in place traverse L to gain groove L of roof (VI). Climb this to ledge on R (20m.). Bridge up the corner on L (VI+) and pass a down pointing flake to reach a ledge. Continue up the corner, strenuous layback (VI+), to a ledge on R (15m.). Steep rock leads L-wards to an easy broken corner and the top (35m.).

51 Magician VI- 110m. ***

This description uses the start of another route, Exterminator, which was destroyed after a rockfall on pitch 2. Start 5m. L of the tree roots.

Climb the easy L wall of a wide shattered corner. Below the 2nd overhang 10m. up, make a difficult step L to the arête. Climb the fine corner above for 20m., and just below a big overhang step L to steep slab, then climb back R with difficulty to regain the wide crack above the roof which is followed to a big ledge on R (45m.). Climb the wide pale corner R of belay by several mantel-shelf moves up the R wall; peg runner in place. From a comfortable ledge on the R make a difficult step L to regain corner; then hand-traverse L to ledges with poor belay; move R and up a nose to a corner. Hand-traverse L and go up steep steps on the L (35m.). An easy ramp bearing L leads to the top (30m.).

150m. R of Magician the walls overhang an extensive pale area of cliff. 70m. L of this part an easier-angled area of rock resembles a semi-circular dome, the top of which is grassy. At the centre of the semi-circle lies the start of Amazing Journey.

52 Amazing Journey V 130m. *

I.Allan, D.Cheesmond, A.Walker, 1975. The easiest good route on Main Wall. Start at an AJ scratched on the rock.

Climb crack diagonally L to ledges and a rocking-block above. Ascend then traverse R and slightly up to an arête. Using tension from a peg and tape (in place) move R round arête to a slab above; climb R to a ledge (40m.). Go up and L over steep broken ground to the base of a steep ramp slanting R; reach this by a steep wall. Go 15m. up ramp to ledge on R below a wide crack system (30m.). Climb crack for 5m., move R below a bulge and descend a few m. to a long ledge with small tree and peg belay in place (20m.). From R end of ledge climb a L-facing corner to its top. Move L at a bulging wall, climb to a ledge system, then R, upwards, and L to the top (40m.).

150m. R of R.52, the long grassy traverses of Dog Leg (move R then L to the top of cliff) provide the easiest route (III) on Main Wall. The next feature to the R is the Central Wall, the highest and most impressive part of the cliffs at Hell's Gate. A

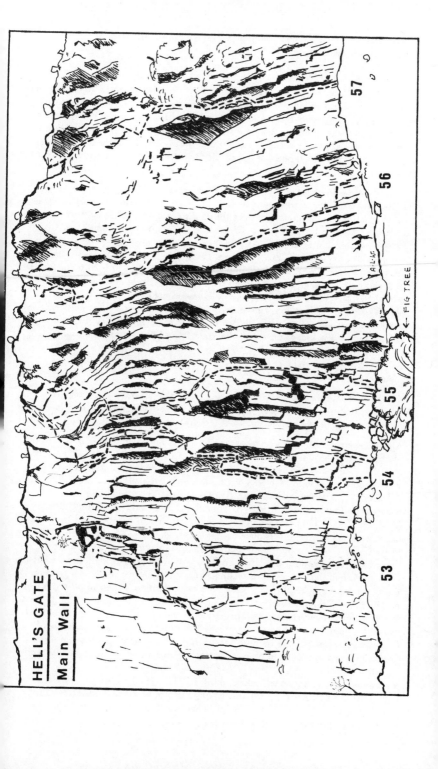

HELL'S GATE

Main Wall

A.L.W.

← FIG TREE

53   54   55   56   57

fine fig tree below its highest sweep grows below grey debris from a recent rockfall.
The best and hardest climbs are located here.

53 Olympian VI-/A1 or VI+ 175m. **

I.Howell, I.Allan, P.Snyder, R.Harper, 1972. The first route to be climbed here.
A popular classic, finding a way through a very steep area of rock seldom exceeding V and providing some fine, exposed climbing. The rotten top band is climbed
by a prominent safe chimney formed by a huge hanging flake. Pitch 5 involves a
strenuous jamming crack, suitable for the big-fisted; its difficulty is out of keeping
with the rest of the climb and the use of aid is justified (several large hexentrics or
no.4 Friends).

25m. L of the L-most boulders in the rockfall area, a R-facing corner leads to a
little cave 15m. up. Climb wall on R for 10m. then traverse L to main chimney-
crack. Climb this to cave and over the roof to ledge on L. Above take fine
parallel cracks to ledge (30m.). Climb to a steep wall, peg runner; go up this
(VI+) then step L into crack. Ascend this, surmount protruding flake, then a
chimney to ledge above (30m.). Trend diagonally L to a large cave (20m.).
Traverse horizontally R to a L-facing rotten corner; follow this to ledge, belay
at R end below a gently overhanging wall (25m.). Climb wall by L-hand jam
crack (VI+ or A1, 10m.). Go R and chimney up behind a flake to a groove.
Step R at top of groove to a fine perch, Lammergeyer Ledge (25m.). Step down
and move R across a slab till a hidden corner is reached. Climb this and the
chimney above to ledges on top of the huge flake (20m.). Finish diagonally L
to the top (15m.).

54 Andromeda VII- 175m. ***

D.Cheesmond, I.Howell, 1975. Takes the Central Wall behind the big fig tree.
The lower pitches provide excellent, sustained climbing. The top pitch is very serious on account of poor rock and lack of protection.

At the L-most point of the great rockfall, climb a pillar to a slab below a line
of overhangs. Move L and surmount these and up to a good ledge (20m.). Go
straight up crack above ledge, hard and off-width near top. Var: step R into
a steep groove; bridge then layback up this with difficulty, moving L to finish.
Belay on top of flake-pillar (VI+, 10m.). Ascend to base of long L-facing
diedre. Follow this direct (VI+) to a small but good belay L of a big flake
(25m.). Climb R over flake and down the other side to a wide crack splitting
buttress on the R. Take this over bulges (VI+), then a rotten chimney, to a big
ledge (30m.). Ignore the corner above; spiral diagonally up buttress on the R
(poor rock) to a ledge. Go L and up 2 steps to a ledge with twin cracks above
(30m.). Climb these (VI-) to a resting place on R. Move up then traverse L to
top of a huge detached pillar. Step up a ramp slanting L (peg in place, VII-)
and climb over bulges to big blocks and good semi-hanging belay (25m.). Move
5m. R on ledges and step up to highest ledge (peg). The original party moved
down from here and traversed several m. R to aid up a groove. Subsequently
parties have climbing the bulging "rock" free above the peg, trending slightly
R (various pegs in place) to gain an arête; finish by a ramp/ledge system leading off R (35m.).
Var. Start. A.Wielochowski, R.Corkhill, 1984. The base of the wide crack
can be reached in 2 direct pitches, giving more pleasant and easier climbing.
Just R of the original start, at a point below the R end of the lowest line of
roofs, climb to a fang pointing down from the roofs; move L to slab above the

fang then traverse 2m. L. Climb jamming crack (VI+, obvious from below), swing L to ledge and belay at top of pitch 2 of original route (35m.). Follow the original line; from base of the dièdre make a long dramatic step R (VI-) to regain the jamming crack. Climb this to base of the wide crack (original pitch 4) and belay 5m. higher, on the L by a peg (15m.).

55 Milky Way VI+ 135m. ***

A.Wielochowski, M.Savage, 1982. Above the fig tree the rockfall has created an area of grey rock capped at 25m. by a band of roofs. The R-most roof has a crack to its R. Start 4m.L of a point directly below crack line, just R of rockfall centre.

Climb dirty rock to a groove and follow this for 5m. Step R across an arête to base of another groove; take this to a roof and move R to a vast semi-detached flake, obvious from below. Follow the fine crack above (VI+) to R end of the roofs (25m.). Continue up crack (VI+) for some 7m., make a thin traverse R to the base of another corner/groove system and climb this to ledges on L. An easy chimney leads to a big ledge (25m.). Take the wall immediately above (V) to gain a slab, traverse L past a dirty crack and round a rotten arête to a comfortable ledge (15m.). Step back R to L side of a great tapering pillar (Shark's Tooth). Climb this then a crack. Above a steep bulge, move L across a steep wall (VI) and mantelshelf onto an excellent ledge (15m.). From L end of ledge move up awkwardly to base of a corner. Climb this (use ledge on R with hidden layaway above, VI) to easier ground and a fine semi-hanging belay 3m. directly above corner (10m.). Traverse R below overhangs using tension from 2 pegs in place and one bolt. Climb white ledges with bulges in between to easier rock and a fine belay on R (VI-, 20m.). Go up to a ledge below a roof; traverse L below a steep rotten wall (various runners including thread) to reach highest ledge, used by roosting birds (peg in place). Reverse down and move L to another ledge system. From a peg in place move L across a dark red wall to an arête; climb this on better rock to a ramp trending R, hence the top (25m.).

56 Zeus VI+, A2 155m. *

I.Howell, M.Savage, I.Allan, 1976. The most impressive feature on Main Wall as viewed from the entrance to the gorge: the great prow or nose 50m. R of the fig tree. The route finishes in a gully well L of nose. On the first acent much aid was used in the serious upper half, and on the 1st pitch; this is now avoided (J.Fantini, 1978). The central aid pitch is unavoidable. Start 10m. R of nose proper, at a recess.

Climb a pillar, move L across a groove, then climb a wall past a bush to horizontal line of holds about 10m. above the ground. Climb 4m. L, moving down across a groove below a roof (difficult) to reach a groove above; climb this till the crack widens. Traverse L below the widening and swing into a groove capped by a roof (old chock). Climb R crack past roof to gain the base of a long fine crack, just R of the nose proper (clearly visible from the ground); this leads to bands of overhangs. Belay 5m. up this (VI+, 40m.). Follow crack to the roof (VI, 25m.). Go up and R (A2, aid mainly in place) to more broken ground, step L across a wall (VI-) and ascend to a ledge with bolt (25m.). Go L and up a slab, then a short steep crack to ledges above. Continue to a peg in a corner, move L then R to reach a pock marked arête and follow this; hand-traverse L and ascend ledges to a steep band (peg, flake and possible belay). Step L from flake to gain pink slabs below the L of 3 overhanging exit corners. Climb to blocks and from a peg and sling in place move down and R, round an arête, to a ledge below the middle corner. Move further R to gain the R corner and a semi-hanging belay (VI, 40m.). Bridge up corner to a ledge leading R to climb a rotten juggy arête to easier ground (V, 30m.).

Just R of Zeus the overhanging walls have been climbed by a serious route: Rocky Horror Show (VI+, A2). 30m. R of Zeus the Central Wall is broken by an obvious line of weakness finishing in a vegetated gully and climbed by Stilleto; this starts directly below in a steep groove L of a grey column.

57 Stilleto V+ 125m. **

Climb crack, go R to ledge and ascend R crack to niche, peg in place (35m.). Bridge up, step R onto buttress and climb to ledge. Move R-wards with difficult route finding to gain a vegetated ramp. Go up L along this to its end (25m.). Climb arête, a ledge then a crack to below overhangs (25m.). From the belay peg move 2m. L and climb through the overhangs (crux). Now traverse R across slabs to finish up gully (40m.). I.Allan, C.Wilson, 1968.

250m. R, the Main Wall changes direction. The Devil Drives uses the area of rock just L of the blunt nose formed by this bend.

58 The Devil Drives V+ 65m. *

I.Allan, A.Walker, 1972. Start below blunt nose on a large block platform.

From detached block climb steep crack to a ledge. Continue up crack then step R and climb blocks to good belay (20m.). Pull up from belay and step R to ledge and so reach a higher ledge; now traverse 5m. L and ascend to a detached block above a small tree; pegs in place on top of block (15m.). A slab direct for 3m. to recess, then climb over bulge to reach a peg. Traverse L to steep cracks; climb the L one to steep broken rock above and the top.

FISCHER'S CLIFF

The low cliff on the R at the entrance of gorge. The lower half provides some excellent problems. Pegs and slings in place about 15m. up provide easy descents.

TOT

This cliff faces you as you drive past the Main Wall going down the gorge. At the L-hand end is a grey buttress with a gully to its L. There are 2 good routes on this buttress. Descent is best by gully R of the routes.

59 Black Widow VI 45m. **

I.Howell, I.Allan, 1973. 10m. L of the nose, a groove entered from the L leads to an obvious small roof at 25m. Below the roof step R and move to steep cracks. Climb these to ledge (30m.). Now climb cracks on R and a chimney to the top (15m.).

60 Black Panther V+ 45m. *

P.Snyder, S.Thumbi, 1972. Start 10m. R of Black Widow. Climb the nose; at 10m. move L into cracks; follow these over bulge to more cracks and an overhang taken direct to ledges (30m.). Move L and climb the crack to its narrowing, then step L onto wall. Go up and back R to finish by a shallow chimney in 15m.

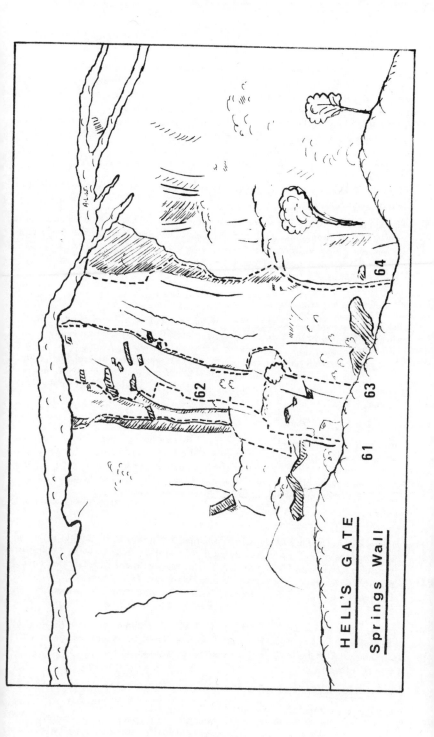

HELL'S GATE

Springs Wall

61

62

63

64

SPRINGS WALL

A few km. down the gorge, Central Tower appears on the L. Just before this on the R is Springs Wall, whose L end is only 80m. from the road and bounded by a deep gully on the L. 50m. R of gully the wall is split by several fine crack lines. On the L a vertical square-cut corner with a roof two-thirds way up is taken by Shadow. Further R, Springer climbs a long crack slanting L to R with a roof at same height. Spider finds a way through the roofs between these 2 routes. Umbra Link begins just L of the nose of the cliff.

61 Shadow   VI+   60m. *

I.Howell, R.Harper, I.Allan, 1970. Scramble up a pillar of boulders leading to a band of overhangs.

Bridge up and step L onto a slab above a roof. Move 2m. L, then go up and R to belay directly below the steep corner (15m.). Climb corner (crux at 6m.), pass a roof and belay on the L, 3m. below the rotten band (25m.). Climb R of the corner to the rotten band. Move L to gain easy but rotten rock and trend L to the top (20m.); belay 20m. higher.

62 Spider   VI-   60m. *

O.Nilssen, A.Wielochowski, 1985. From the boulder pillar of Shadow climb directly up (V+) to the base of a very obvious off-width crack immediately R of pitch 2 of Shadow (15m.). The wide slabby groove just R of the off-width crack is climbed; move R halfway up this, then L to corner where several fine moves L through overhangs lead to a poor stance (25m.). The rotten upper section can either be climbed direct or by moving L to finish on Shadow (20m.); belay 20m. higher.

63 Springer   VI-   70m. *

D.Gray, D.Burkhart, 1971. In centre of this section of crag climb a prominent wide crack to a tree and ledge; step R and climb a short corner. Surmount a bulge, move L across a ledge and climb a steep corner to a grassy ledge (25m.). Gain the long sloping crack; follow this turning roof on R, or taking it direct to a small ledge 4m. higher (30m.). Climb corner direct to top (15m.).

64 Umbra Link   V   85m. **

I.Howell, B.Thomas, 1973. Climb a corner to a grassy ledge on R (15m.). This is just above a big fig tree R of the nose. Steep fine cracks lead to a belay at start of a ramp rising L to R (15m.). Follow ramp with one difficult step through rotten rock to ledge. Traverse L across a black and nearly overhanging wall to a perch on the nose (20m.). Above, take a very steep groove just R of the nose. Step L into a rotten chimney gully and follow this to the top.

There is a bay in the centre of Springs Wall with 2 prominent fig trees growing out of the cliff to the L and above a sandy hollow. Several pleasant and easier routes in this area. R of the bay, one outstanding route provides 3 pitches of varied and sustained climbing.

65 Excelsior Superdirect   VI+   90m. **

Pitch 1 of Superdirect: I.F.Howell, R.J.H.Chambers, 1971. Original (IV) variant: R.J.H.Chambers, D.Burkhart, 1971. Superdirect: T.Jones, A.Wielochowski, 1984. Some 60m. R of the R-most fig tree a huge boulder lies against the cliff with a tiny cave to its L. Above, shattered cracks lead to a pale corner with a crack on the L.

Climb the shattered cracks to a steep short wall; above this climb an easy corner and move R to the arête (30m.). Move back into corner and climb the clean grey corner by a crack on the L (crux at start); where the crack narrows move L over dubious rock to a stance (20m.). Step R and move up over loose-looking blocks to regain the corner. Bridge up this (V) in spectacular position till easy ground leads L to the top.

The original variant crosses the superdirect. It starts 25m. to R and reaches the arête belay of the superdirect in 2 pitches. The grey corner is avoided on the L. The final pitch follows a wide groove directly above the 2nd stance on the superdirect and provides fine exposed straddling to the top.

○ ○ ○ ○ ○

Kitchwa Tembo

TSAVO NATIONAL PARK WEST

General: Climbing first started here in 1978 when Bill Woodley, then the Warden of Tsavo West, opened up the park to climbers and invited the MCK to explore the cliffs. Though difficult to reach, the setting is one of the best in Kenya and the climbing of a high quality. The gneiss walls are often covered in holds and free of vegetation. Cracks and corners abound, but tend to be more vegetated. The most impressive piece of rock, the 300m. high E face, attracted the first explorers and resulted in the ascent of Great Tsavo Chimney. Mastadon took 3 visits before it was completed. One of the latest routes, Ivory Tower on Elephant Rocks, ranks with the best and hardest bush climbs in Kenya.

Generally pegs need not be carried. Unless climbing in the shade, an early start is advisable as it often gets very hot on clear days. The permit the MCK has to climb here, and to camp by the Tsavo river, is a special privilege and every effort must be made not to jeopardize this situation by careless actions. The following should be noted.

(1) Non MCK members must contact the MCK if they wish to climb in Tsavo. At present the privilege is extended to MCK members and their guests only.

(2) A booking fee of KSh 300 must be paid to the park as far in advance as possible. This allows a group to camp at the site for up to 7 days. Bookings are invariably accepted but confirmation by post takes at least 3 weeks. Crossed cheques should be made payable to "The Warden, Tsavo National Park West" and sent to him at PO Box 71, Mtito Andei. Booking inquiries may also be made by radio from the Park HQ, Langata Road, Nairobi (tel. 501081, extn. 32).

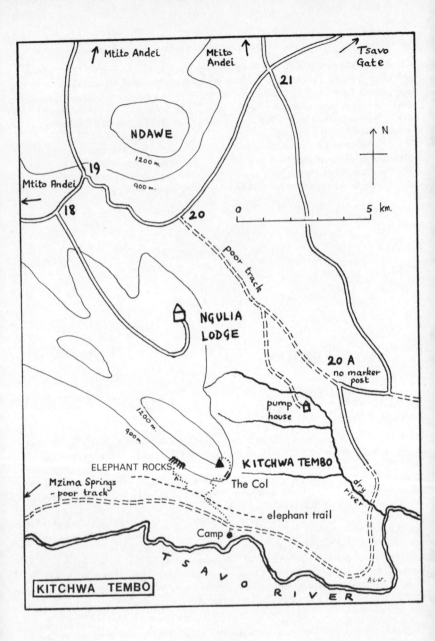

KITCHWA TEMBO

(3) Ensure your vehicle is adequately prepared for the trip. If you do not have 4 WD, planks should be taken to help cope with deep sand.

(4) Do not drive in the park after dark.

(5) No walking, other than to and from climbs, is allowed.

(6) If you require mechanical assistance you will have to walk to Ngulia Lodge where help can be obtained.

(7) Only camp at the designated campsite unless special permission has been given.

(8) Take care with fires and bring out all litter. The toilet is a sandy area W of the camp; go at least 30m. away and dig a deep hole which should be thoroughly filled in after use; a panga should be taken on all trips for this specific purpose.

(9) Do not disturb animals. In the event of any need for medical assistance, obtain help from the warden as soon as possible.

(10) Exercise great care when approaching the river. There are numerous crocodiles and hippopotami in the water whose behaviour is unpredictable. River water can be drunk in an emergency; it contains no major diseases but it is rather muddy. Fresh water is available at the park gates and at Ngulia Lodge.

The nearest petrol/garage facilities are at Mtito Andei, 70 km. from campsite.

Access: Nairobi to the Mtito Andei park gate by road, 230 km. The campsite is still 70 km. ahead. Roads in the park are good and all intersections are clearly marked. From the gate take main road and turn L at the 2nd junction (2A); at the next junction (2B) turn L again. Go straight over the crossroads at 21A where the E face of Kitchwa Tembo is now clearly visible. The track deteriorates; after some 12 km. turn R at an unmarked T junction and soon sharp L at the next unmarked T junction. The campsite is now 12 km. ahead. The track worsens again as it drops towards the Tsavo river. A wide, dry sandy bottomed river is crossed. Drive fast in 2nd gear to avoid getting stuck. Soon after, a similar narrower river bed is crossed. The track then follows the river with no major obstacles. A big boulder stands on R side of the track 150m. before the campsite. Turn L at a point where the river bends away from the track. In 30m. enter shady doum palms beside the river bank. The Col is directly above and Kitchwa Tembo summit lies on a bearing of $5°$ E of N.

Without your own transport access is difficult; numerous buses and matatus run from Nairobi to Mtito Andei at all times of day and night. There is also a train service from Nairobi. However to travel from here to the campsite would involve hiring a vehicle or a taxi in Mtito Andei; this could prove both difficult and costly.

Access to cliffs: All the cliffs are surrounded by dense bush and woods. Dead-fall, vines, thorns, boulders and loose steep soil all combine to impede progress and present difficulties. To minimize these problems choose a route carefully, where possible following animal trails, even if overgrown; if no up/down path exists then traverse till one is found. The access routes described need not be continuous paths, but in their general area there are many animal paths which can be linked together.

ELEPHANT ROCKS

The lowest placed and most accessible cliffs; excellent climbing and popular. A large pointed rock two-thirds way up to the cliffs is a useful route marker. Below and R of this is a tall Baobab tree. Approach this area from the R and, keeping the baobab on your L, aim for the marker rock, passing R of it and coming out just above it. From here a variety of pleasant paths lead to the central grassy bay of Elephant Rocks ($\frac{3}{4}$ h. from campsite). In descent, abseiling from the clifftop is recommended though a traverse L at the top will lead to a poor path down a gully.

The cliffs are split by the giant open-book Ivory Corner, whose L arête is Ivory Tower. The lowest section of cliff just R of this corner is marked by a grassy bay from where routes on the R half of the crag are easily reached. Routes L of Ivory Tower start from a terrace reached by scrambling up a gully 50m. L of grassy bay.

66 Earl Grey IV+ 100m. *

A.Wielochowski, F.Ellyatt, 1981. At the L-most end of the terrace is a R-facing corner, reached by making a short descent before the Tusker start, then traversing.

Just L of a block at base of the cliff climb a crack then traverse L into chimney; tree belay (25m.). Traverse L from chimney onto a steep wall; climb this to a bulge, then traverse R across chimney; climb a wall then move R below over-hangs. Cross a dirty gully and, avoiding chockstones by going R, scramble to a big tree 5m. up gully (30m.). Traverse L below tree along an ever widening ledge, step round a nose and climb slab above, keeping where possible near the L edge (45m.). A fine pitch. Descend in 2 abseils.

67 The Omen V+ 95m. *

A.Wielochowski, 1981. Start at the third corner L of Ivory Corner. Climb a chimney for 4m. and traverse L onto a juggy wall. Climb an arête (hard), move R and L, then follow arête to a stance (40m.). Continue up arête to a ledge with twin cactus trees (20m.). Surmount roof between the cacti, move up then L to arête and at spikes move further L (thin) for 3m. Make 2 moves up then go back R to lip of a roof; climb a crack then a wall and easy slab to the top; cactus belay (45m.). Descent: abseil from a tree 8m. L of top.

68 Tusker IV+ 135m. ***

A.Wielochowski, D.McMullan, R.Corkhill, 1981. Mainly grade III, a few moves of IV+. A beautiful climb.

Start as for The Omen, climb easy rocks R of chimney till a passage leads to base of chimney in the 2nd corner L of Ivory Corner (20m.). The chimney, mainly on R wall, to a slabby ledge on R (15m.). Make an exposed traverse to the arête L (keep low) and go round this to ledge (15m.). Move up and R to reach a spike on arête. From here climb L and up (hard) to reach a black slabby wall. After a few moves make a thin step R to a sandy ledge on arête (pitch 3 could be fin-ished here in order to give the second a top rope on the traverse). Big holds now lead to a horizontal cleft (40m.). Var: a rising traverse at the start of the 3rd pitch leads to spike on the arête which is climbed direct to the cleft (V-, better climbing). Now go over the bulge and follow nose till it steepens. Move R to a juggy wall and go straight up this; cross arête and climb slabs, keeping R where possible, to a commiphora tree at top of corner (45m.). Descend in 2 long abseils from top of corner.

69 White Owl Chimney VI- 125m. *

D.Crowther, A.Wielochowski, 1981. The corner L of Ivory Corner; three sustained chimney pitches and a fine wall finish. Scramble into base of corner from the L.

The chimney to a cramped stance on jammed flakes (25m.); possible to move on to L wall to get a runner. Climb to block overhang, good stance above (25m.). Continue to a runner in the roof then traverse R out of chimney (hard) and bridge up corner to good stance (30m.). Climb corner for 2m. then move R and directly up the wall (hard at first) to move L at top to tree (45m.). Descend by 2 abseils, the first diagonally into the Tusker corner.

70 Exodus VI+ 130m. *

P. O'Sullivan, R. Corkhill, 1981. Pegs useful. The walls R of White Owl Chimney. Halfway up, an obvious bottomless chimney is gained and followed to the top.

Start near R end of terrace and climb a groove to tree at its top (15m.). Move L and climb a shallow groove till a thin traverse R is possible to a scant ledge leading up to a niche (35m.). Follow cracks to ledge and tree (35m.). Climb an overhanging groove till easy ground on L of the fault leads to top (45m.). Descend by abseil starting from a good tree on rim of the L wall of Ivory Corner.

71 Ivory Tower VI+ 200m. ***

A. Wielochowski, I. F. Howell, R. Corkhill, A. Khan, 1982. A serious, sustained climb.

Start one m. L of Ivory Corner and climb a slab directly for 35m. up a brown streak, passing the R-hand end of an overlap at 20m. Traverse 5m. L till easier rock leads to a bushy bay at far R end of terrace (45m.). Step R from bay onto a wall and climb a steepening to loose blocks. Move R, then up and R into Ivory Corner; a messy pitch. Good stance at a pinnacle R of corner (35m.). Place a runner in the corner, move down and swing onto a steep grey slab on L. Traverse L to arête and climb this to a bolt and peg slightly higher. A steep wall (VI+) then jugs lead to a quartz hole and thread runner. Hand traverse L and swing onto a ledge above the big roof. Now L, then up and back R to a small stance on a sloping ledge (30m.). Climb wall above stance for 8m. to a resting place. Move delicately L and up to excellent runners in a crack above a rocking-block. From here climb direct (VII-) to a resting place R of a big detached flake. (This section can be avoided by traversing 3m. L from rocker, climbing (VI+) to a ledge, and R to the detached flake). Bridge up, step R and climb cracks to a ledge below a corner. Bridge up corner to a loose block and roof, traverse L to easier ground and climb to the great horizontal break in the cliff. Belay on white ledge to R, pegs in place (40m.). Surmount roof just L of stance using hidden pocket (protection peg 2m. L), climb good grey rock to a steep wall, move 2m. L, then climb to better holds and a resting place on the R (VI, steep and poorly protected). Ascend 3m. to a better ledge then move 3m. R to easier ground; go up good rock to small stance below a little bulge/ roof (40m.). Climb bulge to easier ground and the top (10m.). Descend as for Ivory Corner.

72 Ivory Corner VI- 200m. **

I. F. Howell, I. Allan, 1980. Named after an elephant tusk found by the first party. Mainly straightforward, airy on the last 2 pitches and vegetated on the pitches in the corner. Easy belaying and an obvious line. Brief description:
Start 20m. L of central grassy bay at a groove with tree. Climb crack for 65m., vegetated in parts, till the L wall overhangs; take an overhanging jamming crack (crux), keeping out on the slabby R wall wherever possible. Easy chimneys above lead to the upper sections of the corner where the chimney becomes unpleasantly wide and is adorned with hornets nests. From just below the highest

tree in corner proper, traverse L then move up into a bay. Trend R to a small R-facing corner and climb this to a belay. Take the crack above to top. From a tree near the finish several abseils down the corner lead to the bottom.

The arête R of Ivory Corner is climbed by Ivory Pillar (VI-, A1); near the top a slab L of pillar is taken. R of this is another huge corner system. The top sections of the L-hand walls are red and overhanging. A giant roof caps the whole system. The corner and slabs to the R are climbed by Call of the Wild (V+). About 20m. R of this the slab overhangs a groove line slanting R which starts in a cave and initially is dirty and overhanging; great blocks are jammed in it a few m. up.

73   Vampire   VI   200m. **

A.Wielochowski, R.Corkhill, 1983. Though rather devious, gives varied climbing of high quality. Start just R of cave, on top of a pedestal formed by a huge fallen block resting against the cliff.

Climb slab just R of pedestal or move up from pedestal to a white crack (runner) and traverse R onto slab. Climb this to top of the white crack (VI-). Traverse L and down (good holds below the overlap) to gain a stance on the jammed blocks (15m.). Jam then hand traverse L (VI-) to reach a groove slanting R. Climb this to stance above a grassy ledge (15m.). Continue up slanting crack for 6m. to chockstones (runner). Above, the crack widens to a chimney; below this step L onto a steep wall. Move up to a big hold, mantelshelf onto this (VI+), move L then climb an easy slab to a tree (20m.); from here one abseil reaches the bottom. Traverse R for 2m., climb a slabby wall till a break leads R into a grassy bay; above this traverse further R across a blank slab to reach grooves leading up to R-hand end of a roof line. Small stance several m. below roof (30m.). Climb to a corner R of the roof and take this till it is possible to traverse out L, round a nose and to a corner on L below cactuses and a small tree (25m.). Climb past cactuses to a roof (Shifta comes in here from the R); take a tapering slab above to reach a horizontal cleft splitting the cliff at half height (25m.). Move slightly L, pull over the roof of cleft (difficult) to a slight recess on R. Climb this (peg runner) to easier slabs and go up these keeping slightly L to a ledge and belays in a wide crack (35m.). Follow this crack, breaking out L where it steepens. Move up, then back R into the now thin crack and go L across a slab to climb a wall to easy ground. Descend by abseiling down Ivory Corner.

74   Shifta   V+   200m. **

A.Wielochowski, D.McMullan, 1981. R of Vampire the slabs are unbroken till another major slightly vegetated fault is reached. From a pedestal just L of this fault climb to a high runner to protect a thin traverse R across a black slab, to gain the start of the fault line by tree roots and above a roof. Climb past two trees then an awkward traverse leads R to the arête; go up this to a ledge (45m.). Climb arête then move L and up a clean crack just R of a chimney. Take a stance before the crack ends (25m.). Take the R wall, step L across the corner and go up more easily till a long traverse L across the steep wall leads over an arête to a tapering slab (Vampire). Climb this (crux) to the horizontal cleft (25m.). Crawl L to a stance near trees (10m.). Surmount the roof at a point 20m. directly below the R-most end of the giant roof on the L; climb to this, passing it just to the R. Trend R to ledge and belays in a wide crack (40m.). Now as for pitch 8 of Vampire. Descend as for Vampire.

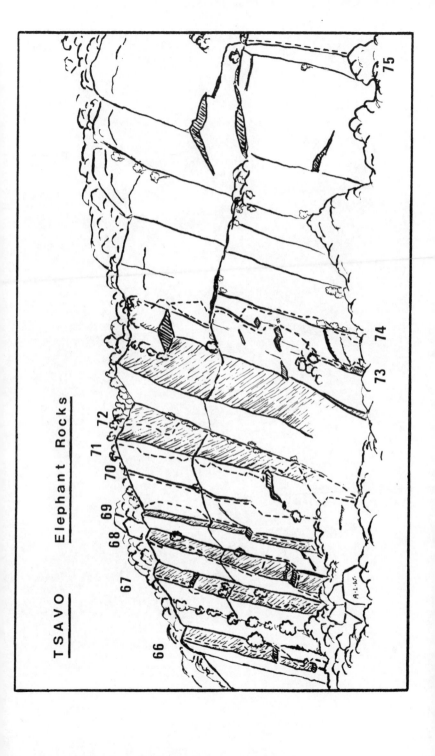

TSAVO   Elephant Rocks

66 67 68 69 70 71 72 73 74 75

Earl Grey on Elephant Rocks, Kitchwa Tembo.

Tusker on Elephant Rocks, Kitchwa Tembo.

Ivory Tower on Elephant Rocks, Kitchwa Tembo.

R of Shifta several routes climb the crack systems to the horizontal fault and slabs above. All are good. The R end of this cracked area ends in a long black corner, leading up to a vegetated bay below the L end of a long overhang above the horizontal cleft which splits the cliff. Beyond this the base of cliff drops, and R of a blunt nose a sweep of black slabs appears. Several climbs start here. The R end is bounded by a L-facing chimney system, vegetated in its upper half. At the bottom a big fig tree grows out of the R wall of the corner, 5m. above the ground.

75 Arc of a Diver IV 100m. **

G.Hornby, D.Crowther (soloing), 1981. The blunt arête above the fig tree and R of the corner. A delightfully open slab climb, very popular and the easiest route in the area; rarely exceeds III+.

Start 20m. beyond the buttress nose, below and R of fig tree, at a long, wide L-trending crack; climb this to belay on top of a pinnacle (15m.). Var: climb direct, starting below the fig tree. Now the wall above pinnacle, R then L, to slabs; climb a crack and belay near its top (15m.). Follow rib to an overhang (unprotected), turn this on R and at next overhang traverse L to a tree (45m.). Gain the top of overhang from L side. Follow nose to the top (15m.).
An interesting descent from this route is via the Bat Cave. At the top go 3m. R and descend onto a lower overhung ledge system leading into the cave. At the other end a window leads to top of an easy gully; scramble down this for a few m., till it is possible to traverse R (facing cliff) and across into a waterworn gully leading to the bottom.

Immediately L of Elephant Rocks a vegetated descent gully is bounded to its L by a great fin of rock. The arête of this fin is covered in green lichen and has vertical seams. Monkey Arête (V+ **) climbs this (keeping R where possible) on good rock.

KITCHWA TEMBO

A fine summit though difficult to reach. The Nose and E face provide some of the best climbing in Tsavo. The Col lies SE of the summit below the second step; an almost continuous path leads from the camp to the Col, but it is difficult to find or to follow and stay on. The general directions indicated below should be adhered to. From the camp aim for the L end of Elephant Rocks along a good game trail. From a slight saddle below the main rise take the open slopes, aiming just R of the summit. Low on this slope 2 big boulders can be seen; the lower resembles a R-facing rabbit. Aim to pass these at a point 100m. to their R then trend L-wards. Shortly the slope becomes covered in big boulders and tall trees; traverse L along a good path at this level for 50m. Cross the main gully and take its L side till a traverse R leads back across it and up to a waterslide. At the top go R and take a path up to a grassy area R of big shady trees. The path zigzags up and works to R towards the Col ($1\frac{1}{4}$ h. from camp, 45 min. in descent).
The E face can be reached in a further 30 min. Walk 40m. N from the Col then drop down an ill defined path for 50m. Now make a long traverse towards the E face, gaining height where possible. Var: follow ridge of R.76, to scramble down and abseil from a block below the Falcon cracks. Fine biv. site at boulders below the Great Tsavo Chimney.
Descent is best taken down the vegetated, unpleasant South Gully (I), reached by going NW from the summit down open slabs to a flat col. Immediately push L to attain head of the thickly vegetated gully. 100m. down, a traverse R is made to a ridge. Descend R side of this for 200m., then traverse back into gully, now

followed more easily to bottom (45 min.). Work down and L (facing outwards) to regain path to the Col. An alternative descent involves turning E at flat col below summit and descending slabs then a gully on the L (abseils) to bottom. Then a thickly vegetated traverse leads in about 15 min. to the biv. boulders.

76 Covenant IV+ 105m. ***

I.Howell, I.Allan, 1981. An expedition of great character and exposure. At the Col follow the alpine-style ridge to foot of the lower nose of Kitchwa Tembo.

Climb a chimney, step L and shortly move back R into chimney; go up for 3m., move L onto the arête and up to small cave stance (35m.). The chimney to a platform at top (20m.); the L wall can be climbed in the middle section of this pitch. Step R (thread runner) and climb a quartz band, moving R on slabbier ground to belay block on nose (20m.). Now L across slabs, then easier rock leads to ridge (30m.). Var: the quartz band can be climbed direct (excellent, VI-). Follow ridge across a crevice to base of the final step. Either climb this (The Link), or scramble down a gully on L for 40m. to a tree on the R wall, from where a 45m. abseil leads into South Gully. It is also possible to abseil down the climb itself.

77 Great Tsavo Chimney V+ 200m. **

A.Wielochowski, M.Savage, 1978. A superb chimney climb; long pitches of fine bridging on good rock. The line is obvious, briefly as follows.
Enter chimney with difficulty, then 2 ways are evident for the 2nd pitch: at a narrowing, climb face to L (VI-) till it is possible to regain chimney, or avoid the face by going deep into chimney and climbing in semi-darkness (IV). The 4th pitch involves a hard move L round a chockstone (V+). Near the top stay on the outside of chimney. For continuations, see Covenant.

L of R.77 another chimney splits the E face but does not reach the ground. Falcon (well-protected, exposed, VI- **) climbs this area of rock: a slab leads to base of the wall which is climbed by steep cracks trending R. A ramp system slanting to R leads to the chimney which is followed for 5m., then a slab on R leads to a hidden ledge with tree; steep cracks above L end of ledge lead to the top.

78 The Link VI- 65m. **

A.Wielochowski, R.Corkhill, 1981. A fine continuation to Covenant, the Great Tsavo Chimney or Falcon, taking steep exposed slabs R of the headwall. Although not technically hard, the poor belay, sparse protection, difficult route finding and complex rope handling make this a serious route.

Step across Great Tsavo Chimney to a ledge; move 2m. R to a spike then climb direct to a grassy ledge on L and poor belay, peg (10m.). Move R onto slabs and climb these trending initially slightly R; after 2 mantelshelf moves, go L and down across a holdless slab to reach easier ground above. If climbing on a double 9mm. rope it is best now to untie from one of them, join them together and continue up the much easier ground to a belay a long way back (55m.).

The next 2 routes are situated on the E face proper. Both provide excellent wall climbing rarely exceeding V-. Belays and protection however need a lot of care. A small selection of pegs is recommended for Mastadon.

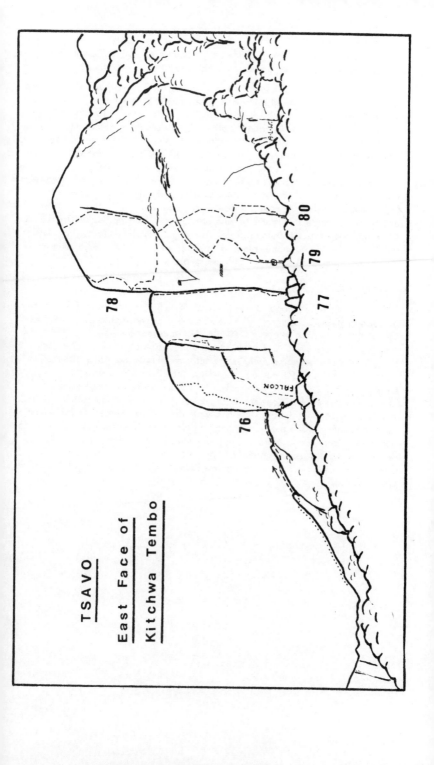

TSAVO

East Face of
Kitchwa Tembo

76 77 78 79 80

FALCON

79 <u>Mastadon</u> VI+ 310m. **

A.Wielochowski, P.O'Sullivan, I.Howell, R.Corkhill, 1981. Start R of the biv. boulders, where a tree 10m. up has roots hanging down to the ground.

Climb the roots then a chimney to a small niche (35m.). Go up to a overhang, traverse 3m. R onto a blunt arête and follow this to a steepening. Traverse back L to a corner (30m.). Go back R then up diagonally R till a line of holds is taken diagonally L (hard), then a wall to a small L-facing corner and hanging belay below a ledge (30m.). From ledge go L then 5m. direct to big holds. So L again (difficult) to runners, then up 2m. and L again. Several more L-then-up moves lead to a ramp which crosses face from L to R. Belay on ramp, L of a thin semi-detached rock pillar, pegs (40m.). Climb ramp to a good ledge (45m.). Go up diagonally L across slabs to top of a second, higher ramp line; block belay (25m.). Move up then R following an arching crack to reach a grassy overhang; surmount this (hard) to base of a chimney cutting the headwall (25m.). Climb chimney to small ledge (35m.). The chimney narrows to a crack; bridge over narrowing into a niche (runners), step onto L wall and climb a slab above trending L (45m.). A sustained and poorly protected pitch.

80 <u>Behemoth</u> VI 295m. ***

M.Savage, A.Wielochowski, 1981. Start 40m. R of Mastadon, at the bottom of a long L-facing chimney. Climb this for 6m., traverse onto wall R and take this over a bulge to a big ledge (40m.). Go up direct for 40m. first trending L then R. Traverse 6m. L to a ledge above a band of roofs (45m.). The next belay is directly above on a big ledge and can be reached either directly, or more easily by moving L and up to a spike, then back R and straight up, pegs (45m.). Climb L on easier slabs; after 20m. pass the belay ledge at end of the Mastadon ramp pitch. Continue to block belay as for Mastadon pitch 6 (45m.). Traverse horizontally L below the headwall till you can almost see the Great Tsavo Chimney. Take the wall above (unprotected) till a hard move L leads to a hanging belay from a spike and nut, level with top of Great Tsavo Chimney (45m.). Ascend to easier ground and go up L to a ledge overlooking the top of Great Tsavo Chimney, some 12m. below (30m.). Continue as for pitch 2 of The Link (55m.).

Ndeiya

General: A line of small outcrops situated slightly further from Nairobi than Embaribal. The climbing, birdlife and situation is not as good as at Embaribal, but the style is similar, the access to routes easier and locating them is greatly assisted by numbers painted on the rock. Temperatures are pleasant at most times and there is often a cool breeze. Facing E, it is coolest in the afternoon. Small campsite among boulders and trees below Central Crag. Garage facilities and water are available at Ngong town (25 km.).

Access: As for Embaribal to the small church. At this junction turn R. After 4.7 km. ignore a turn off L to a rifle range. Continue for 1.5 km. to another turn off L; again take the R fork and follow this for 6 km. to the start of the rocks. The first major outcrop is Red Crag, followed by a broken area. Central Crag is located 600m. R of Red Crag. A rough track turns off at a point directly opposite the descent gully on R side of Central Crag; this leads in 150m. to campsite. Matatus rarely pass the rocks.

Red Crag is prominent at the S end of the cliff line. The first 3 routes are located here.

81 Giant's Steps IV 45m.

R.Chambers, G.Hodges, R.Pillinger, 1964. A pleasant route. After the first move the climbing is III. At L end of crag, note large R-facing corner. Start 5m. R of this below a wide crack (painted, 1). Attain crack with difficulty (shoulder ?) and climb it to block at top (15m.). Walk L to end of big ledge (7m.). Climb a chimney-crack, walk to L end of a ledge and climb past small tree to a big ledge (16m.). An obvious crack in wall behind (7m.).

82 May Day V 30m.

M.Harris, C.&J.Powell, 1966. An escapable line with some excellent moves. R of R.81 note a big fig tree at base of crag. About 30m. further R a vast slab lies on the ground below cliff. Start 10m. further R in a corner, with several rock pillars standing close to base (painted 5,6,7). Climb a steep corner to loose-looking rock below a big roof; 2m. below roof step R to a rounded block below the chimney line bordering roof to R (4m. directly above a big fig tree growing out of the cliff). Step R and up then L to a corner and resting place. Go up for 2 moves, then layback to a sloping ledge (25m.). Continue to layback to the top (5m.).

L of May Day and starting from top of a pinnacle, Gog (III) climbs a clean R-facing corner, then a slab to a cave and finishes by an athletic move. Immediately R of May Day, a line of polished cracks leads R to just above the fig tree mentioned in May Day, then climb to a 2nd tree; from this go straight up via a narrow chimney to top (Harambee, III+). 13m. R of May Day, a white root hangs down an overhang halfway up cliff. Below this is the start of Plumb.

83 Plumb IV+ 30m. *

J.Mbithi, 1965. A fine sustained route. Climb a shallow chimney to the root, move up then swing R to a ledge and climb more easily to regain the crack above overhang after 2m. Follow this to the top.

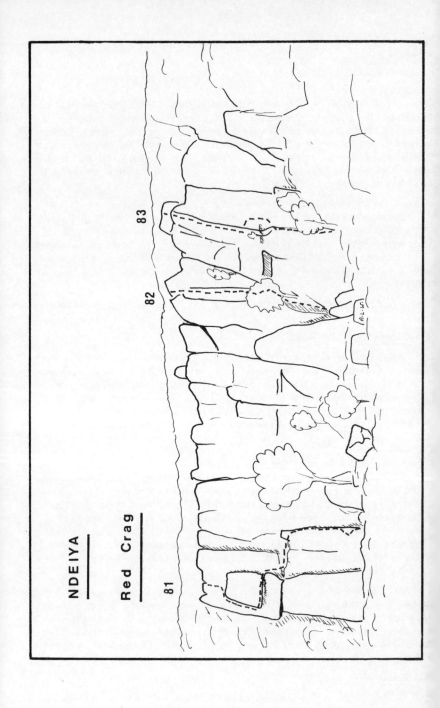

NDEIYA

Red Crag

81   82   83

The following are all on Central Crag. Immediately above the campsite a fine tall buttress has 3 grooves cutting it. The central one is taken by Party Grooves and is painted 43; one of Ndeiya's best climbs. 25m. L of this a vast block forms a tunnel and chimney at base of the crag. Here starts Morning Shade (painted 40). 75m. further L a similar block lies against the cliff forming a chimney and passage. L of this is the start of Ridge Way (IV+ *). Fracture starts in the chimney – one of the best easier climbs; painted 32 and 33 respectively.

84 Fracture IV 30m. **

P.Carslake, R.J.H.Chambers, 1964. Pleasant, well protected, varied and on clean rock. Climb chimney, exiting at top through hole. Now L side of a pillar up fractured blocks; belay on a pinnacle (15m.). Traverse R across wall to gain ledge with tree (5m.). The corner above, taken direct with fine jamming to top (10m.). Or finish up an easier wide crack on the R (III *).

From just below the pinnacle belay on Fracture an excellent alternative is to climb the top pitch of Ridge Way; hand traverse L and mantelshelf onto a ledge on the ridge. Follow ridge to the top (III+).

30m. R of Fracture in a shady bay between boulders and trees, a steep corner leads to a slab with caves and nests below big overhangs. Veerog (VI- *) starts at base of a groove (painted 36); some fine moves and positions on this climb, but the 1st pitch (originally aided) is now unpleasantly free; after the groove traverse a steep slab R-wards to gain a ridge; climb a slab on R to a small tree. Above this balance into a corner on L and climb this past a tree to the top.

85 Morning Shade IV 45m. *

R.J.H.Chambers, H.Mwongela, 1964. Pleasant but rather bitty and not well protected on 1st pitch. The chimney to R-most chockstone, then corner on R to a big fig tree (15m.). Move L, go up then L again to gain short corner with a root; climb this to a 2nd big fig tree. A pleasant corner on R to big platform (18m.). Climb a corner L of platform to the top (12m.).

L of Morning Shade rises an overhanging prow called The Mummy. Just L of this a steep corner, and L again a shallow chimney leading after 5m. to a ledge: above this the chimney divides. The R half has a repulsive roof, the L a projecting block. The L one gives a pleasant climb (Cliff's Route, IV *) which turns the projecting block L. 15m. R of Morning Shade is the start of Crackpot (VI, painted 42), being the L-most of the 3 obvious main grooves of the Central Buttress. Just R of this is:

86 Party Grooves VI 50m. ***

M.S.Harris, J.Powell, R.J.H.Chambers, 1966. Sustained, fine climbing. Start at the painted 43 and climb a steep slab on poor rock to an obvious crack breaking through bulges above. Climb crack (peg runners, crux) to a ledge below the corner proper. Go up this initially using the R wall till a step L leads to a ledge and belays on L (25m.). Step R into corner and climb the groove, overhanging at first; at a chockstone climb the R wall then continue to the top (25m.).

Just R of the slab start of Party Grooves is a small, short R-facing corner, marking start of the next route.

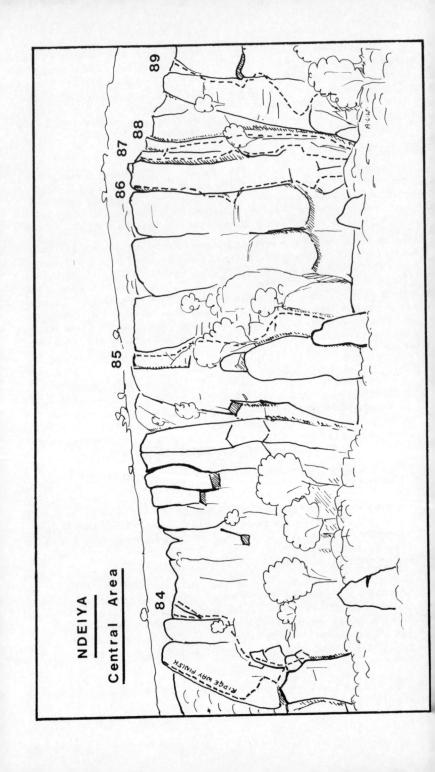

87 Nutcracker VI+ 45m. ***

At the painted numbers 44,45 and 46, climb to a bulge and surmount it by a shallow crack to a resting ledge. From R side of this a short R-facing corner leads to base of groove proper. Take it by a steep, strenuous jamming crack. Belay on a ledge above and on R (25m.). Move R and up to a ledge in the next corner; step back L to finish by the main corner (20m.). A direct finish is a fine, sustained and well protected pitch climbing the main corner through-out.

88 Knight's Move V+ 45m. *

R.Pillinger, R.Baillie, 1964. The description below is a more pleasant variation of the original way which, above the tree belay of pitch 1, moves up and traverses R across a smooth wall and slab (with the help of a sapling) to gain a tree and hence the top.

Start one m. R of Nutcracker (painted 45,46,47). Climb a crack up the wall, then take the R of twin cracks to big tree above (25m.). Reach a ledge on the nose to L (tree not required). Climb to a corner, then to a ledge below a very steep corner (15m.). Step L from ledge to top part of the steep corner which is the finish of Nutcracker Direct; take this to the top.

89 Surprise IV+ 45m. **

M.S.Harris, R.J.H.Chambers, 1966. A good route. A few m. R of Knight's Move are several trees at base of the cliff; start in a deep corner behind the first tree and climb the cracked corner on good jams, then bridge onto an easy slab on L. Climb steep blocks then move R across ledge to belay (25m.). Now a steep crack to overhang; turn this by mantelshelf on L and climb to a ledge and thread belay (12m.). The R crack to top (8m.).

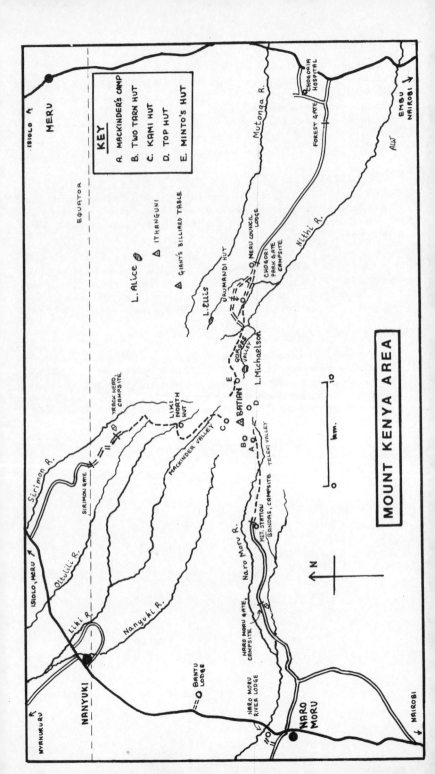

MOUNT KENYA AREA

MOUNT KENYA

GENERAL

MOUNT KENYA (5199m.) is the second highest mountain in Africa. Although it lies only a few km. from the Equator, it is heavily glaciated. The summit area consists of numerous smaller peaks surrounding the 2 main peaks of Nelion and Batian. The majority of these are composed of syenite, a superb rough rock for climbing. The whole mountain area is a National Park and the walk in through forest and moorland is for many visitors the most pleasant part of the trip. Climbers are strongly recommended to adopt a leisurely pace. Acclimatization problems on Mt. Kenya are underestimated by many parties; they rush up to the peaks in one day and find themselves too sick to climb. There have been many cases of pulmonary oedema, mainly as a result of high altitudes being reached too fast. In the event of pulmonary oedema rapid descent is imperative.

To ascend the highest summits requires technical rock and snow climbing of at least grade IV (severe) standard, and many parties bivouac on the mountain. The third highest peak, Pt. Lenana (4985m.), can be reached by walkers and is ascended by hundreds of people each year.

The flora and fauna of the park is very rich. The forest zone is inhabited by buffalo and elephant and care should be taken when these are encountered (see Intro.). Hyrax, related to the elephant but looking more like an overgrown rat minus the long tail, and various rodents inhabit the moorland. These scavangers will dig up litter or rummage through tents in search of food. For this reason do not leave food lying around. Carry all litter off the mountain and do not bury it.

The weather has been discussed in the introduction. Even in the best season (end December to mid-March) there are periods of 2 or 3 days when the weather might be bad, and snowfall could prevent rock climbing. After several wet days access roads in the park may be closed to avoid damage to them, and the moorland paths can become very boggy – particularly on the Naro Moru and Sirimon routes.

The usual walking access routes are: (i) The Naro Moru, the normal tourist and fastest way up to the southern peak area. A good vehicle track leads to 3000m. and from this roadhead the peak area can be reached in about 7h. (ii) The Sirimon and (iii) The Chogoria; these are longer, scenically more rewarding, less used and less developed. The Chogoria is especially beautiful. (iv) Other routes include the Kamweti from the S and the Timau from the N. Also the 3 Bantu Lodge routes provide magnificent wilderness walks through unspoilt forest and moorland.

Another fine expedition is the "Round the Peaks" walk. It provides a circular tour linking the main access routes. Walking on the main routes, though physically demanding, is generally straightforward and paths are well marked. Access routes to climbs often skirt near the edges of glaciers where their recession has left precariously balanced and potentially dangerous boulders. The Krapf glacier below the E face of Nelion is particularly bad.

Huts on the mountain are generally small and dirty. Camping is recommended, though this does mean heavier sacks.

Facilities available on the 3 main access routes and costs per man night are as follows. Naro Moru route, at the 3000m. roadhead, clean and pleasant bandas (100 KSh) or it is possible to camp (15 KSh extra to park charges). In the Teleki Valley, Mackinder's Camp provides tents with mattresses (80 KSh) but these are gradually being removed as the bunkhouse (160 KSh) is being brought into use;

camping here is possible (15 KSh extra to park charges). A small hut located in the Teleki Valley is for the exclusive use of MCK members (free). On the Sirimon route, good campsites at the roadhead, by the Liki North Hut (small and often dirty) and near Shipton's Caves. On the Chogoria route there are very comfortable, self-catering bandas (Meru Mt. Kenya Lodge) beside the park gate (160 KSh.). A short walk from the gate, climbers may prefer to use the Urumandi Hut. This hut and the bandas are situated in the picturesque "Parklands" which abound in game and offer many short walks in the neighbourhood. Several good campsites near the roadhead, and beside Minto's Hut – itself small and rather dirty.

The charge for MCK huts is 20 KSh. Bookings for any of these (other than MCK hut in Teleki Valley) should be done through one of the following: the Naro Moru River Lodge, PO Box 18, Naro Moru, tel. Naro Moru 23. The Alliance Hotels, College House, PO Box 49839, Nairobi, tel. 337501. Let's Go Travel, PO Box 60342, Nairobi, tel. 29539, 29540 or 340331. The Meru Mt. Kenya Lodge is booked exclusively through Let's Go Travel. Roadhead facilities on the Naro Moru route together with Mackinder's Camp are booked through the Alliance Hotels or Naro Moru River Lodge. Halfway from Naro Moru to the park gate, on the L side of the road, is a Youth Hostel; clean and pleasant.

Naro Moru River Lodge provides bandas in Naro Moru, equipment hire, transport to and from the 3000m. roadhead (700 KSh per vehicle journey, one way) and will organize guides and porters (approx. 150 KSh per load carried to the Teleki Valley). Bantu Lodge (PO Box 333 Nanyuki, tel. Burguret 1) just N of Naro Moru offers similar facilities, with good porters and guides, at a lower price.

Porter and guide services on the mountain have not been too reliable and efforts are being made to smarten-up their organization. The Naro Moru route porters are based 7 km. from the lodge on road to the gate. For guides and porters serving the Chogoria route contact Mount Kenya Transversers Ltd, PO Box 83, Chogoria, tel. Meru 20781/2.

Park fees have to be paid at the park gates as follows: Entrance 30 KSh; camping 5 KSh per night; vehicle 30 KSh. All park gates have radio contact with each other and the Park Rescue/Ranger post the Teleki Valley. Camping is possible at all gates and water is available.

Food for the mountain should be bought in Nairobi. Water is plentiful and with few exceptions is clean. Water from the Kami Tarn should be collected at inflow (SW). Garage facilities are available at Naro Moru, Nanyuki (for Sirimon route) and Chuka near Chogoria village.

ACCESS

Naro Moru Route: Tarmac roads lead to Naro Moru, 170 km. from Nairobi. The park gate at 2400m. is 17 km. from Naro Moru along a good dirt road. Among bus and matatu services to Naro Moru, the MPS (based in Nairobi) is particularly reliable. From Naro Moru matatus only go part way to the gate; a ride on passing vehicles can be tried. From the gate it is occasionally possible to get a lift to the 3000m. roadhead. See also the Naro Moru River Lodge vehicle service mentioned above.

Sirimon Route: Tarmac roads to Nanyuki. Continue 15 km. N on tarmac and at a signpost turn R onto a dirt road leading to the Sirimon Gate (2700m.) in 10 km. Buses, matatus and the MPS ply the tarmac road. From the turning to the Sirimon Gate, failing a lift one must walk.

Chogoria Route: Tarmac roads to Chogoria, then a dirt road for 9 km. to the forestry gate, and in a further 22 km. the park gate and Meru Mt. Kenya Lodge bandas are reached at 2900m. Good bus and matatu services to Chogoria. Chogoria Rider (based in Nairobi) offers the most convenient service. From Chogoria a lot of luck would be needed to get a lift to the park gate. It is possible to book a Land Rover to take you from the Chief's Camp to the gate; this costs 450 KSh and the booking should be made through The Manager, Meru Mt. Kenya Lodge, PO Box 365, Chogoria.

Bantu Lodge routes: The lodge lies one km. off the main tarmac road and 5 km. from Naro Moru town; it is the best base for the Bantu Lodge routes (check on status of these beforehand). Transport to the roadheads costs 600 KSh per journey.

APPROACHES

1. Naro Moru Route: to S side of Mt. Kenya.
Well marked throughout. The "Vertical Bog" is often the rather unpleasant, muddy crux of the walk. From the park gate (2400m.) the track rises through splendid forest for 9 km. to the Meteorological Station (3000m.) and roadhead for private cars ($3\frac{1}{2}$ h. on foot). Radio contact with gate; possible to store equipment with a caretaker. Continue up track beyond barrier to top of the forest. Now go up the Vertical Bog (marker posts) till a drier ridge leads to a vantage point commanding the Teleki Valley (4000m.). No water on this leg (4 h.). Either take the low level trail, soon crossing the Naro Moru stream (possible campsite); or the high trail, more scenic but swampy in wet weather. Continue up the valley till a path ascends from the floor to a hidden flat area on the L where Mackinder's Camp (4200m.) is located. The scenic route crosses the stream to meet the path leading off L to Mackinder's Camp. A short way up the valley, on the L, is the Ranger Post with a radio mast beside it. Numerous pleasant campsites along the stream ($1\frac{1}{2}$ h.); the nights here are very cold. Walking in the early morning is pleasant as the boggy areas are frozen.

   Now ways diverge. Two Tarn Hut (4490m.) can be reached by following a steep trail diagonally up and N from the Ranger Post. The hut is small with good campsites nearby (2 h.). For Top Hut (4490m.) take the main path from the Ranger post, traverse NW side of valley and cross the Naro Moru stream to the R side. The trail goes up long screes and zigzags to finish on a ridge before reaching the hut; spacious but bleak (3 h.).

   From the Ranger Post again, instead of crossing the stream, a gently rising path just L of a low, bouldery moraine ridge, follows L side of the valley to the highest flat, grassy area – American Camp (4320m., 1 h.). Above this screes rise to a terminal moraine below the snout of the Tyndall Glacier (possible bleak campsite at the Tyndall Tarn). Scree and easy rocks on the R lead to a flat bouldery area at 4600m. between the Darwin Glacier and Pt. John; so reach base of this glacier (1 h. from American Camp). Just S of tiny ponds a good shelter can be found under a boulder. From here the foot of the Normal Route on Mt. Kenya or Top Hut could be reached by scrambling over the col (4649m.) between Midget Peak and Pt. John, traversing below the sheer walls of Pt. John, then crossing screes on the NW side of the Lewis Glacier (cairned) – either crossing the glacier to Top Hut, or rising to foot of the Normal Route.

2. Sirimon Route: to N side of Mt. Kenya.
Here is some of the best forest walking in the park; a long hike crossing a high ridge while the Mackinder Valley can be boggy in wet periods. From the park gate a track winds up to roadhead at 3350m. in the moorland; campsite and water. Saloon

cars can get most of the way, and 4 WD vehicles all the way, unless the track is very wet (4 h.). Follow the gradually deteriorating track till a horizontal traverse R is made; cross a small stream, gain a ridge top and descend into the Liki North Valley. One km. up the valley, on the W side, is the Liki North Hut (3940m.), a small, often dirty building with pleasant campsites nearby (3½ h.). Shortly before the hut a path rises diagonally W over the hillside to cross a ridge at 4180m., then drops SW into the Mackinder Valley. After one km. it crosses the stream and passes R of a band of rocks. Near the L end of these is located a poor shelter, Shipton's Cave (4050m.), with good campsites before and after it (2¾ h.).

The route divides. One way goes S, rising high above the valley floor to reach Kami Hut and its Tarn (4439m.); campsites nearby (1¾ h.). By following the main stream SE, Simba Col (4620m.) is attained. From here it is possible to reach Top Hut by a long traverse round the E and S faces of Lenana, or to descend to Minto's Hut and the Chogoria Route.

3. Chogoria Route: to E side of Mt. Kenya.

The most spectacular approach to the main peaks, with beautiful views into the Gorges Valley. From the forest gate at 1700m. follow good track for 22 km. in the forest to the park gate at 2900m. (9 h.). Now by a vehicle track towards the Kinithi River and after a few hundred m. take a turn off L. Go down and cross the stream. Then the Urumandi Hut (3063m.) is reached in about 30 min. (1 h.). Cross a natural bridge over the stream below the hut and follow a path upstream to reach the track-head and a small campsite by the Nithi North stream at 3300m. A fine waterfall 100m. below campsite (1 h.).

It is possible to walk directly to the roadhead by taking the main vehicle path (R fork) to the Kinithi River. Cross this and follow the main trail to reach the road-head in 2 h. from the park gate.

Cross the stream and gain a ridge. Follow the well-marked path to Minto's Hut (4270m.), beside Hall Tarn (campsite) in a magnificent situation. No water on this leg (5 h.). The path continues up the valley and finally climbs steeply on scree to reach Simba Tarn, just below Simba Col (1½ h.). This is a good start point for the N ridge of Lenana.

Various ways to continue. From Simba Col a traverse W leads in just over 1 h. to Kami Hut. Keep high initially, then drop down a moraine ridge and lastly take a well-cairned traverse over scree and boulders to hut. From Simba Tarn a traverse S over a col, then E, leads in 2 h. to Top Hut. By going straight down NW from Simba Col the Sirimon route is reached.

4. Bantu Lodge approaches:

Three unspoiled routes have been developed. As they are new and poorly defined it is important to obtain more information and possibly a guide and porters from the Bantu Lodge.

a) The Burguret route is a reopened old mule trail up to Two Tarn Hut. Good 4WD vehicles can reach a campsite at 2990m. in dry weather. A faint path (boggy in wet weather) continues up to The Highland Castle (cave shelters, 3650m.), then along the Burguret River (campsites between 3700m. and 4100m.), to swing L then up to Two Tarn Hut (a very long day from roadhead). Var: at 4000m. a long traverse R leads into the Teleki Valley.

b) The New Bantu route is much drier with some fine walking in parkland scenery. Good campsites at 3100m. and at c.3800m. Higher up the ridge above the Teleki Valley can be followed to Two Tarn Hut or an easy traverse leads into the valley itself (8 h. from 2750m. roadhead to Mackinder's Camp).

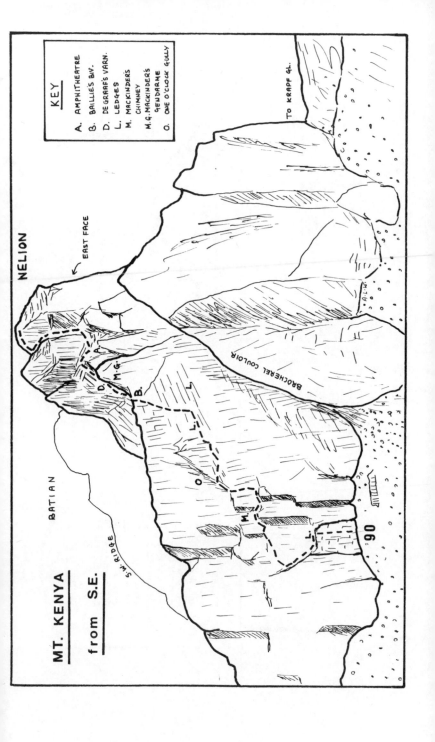

MT. KENYA

from S.E.

NELION

← EAST FACE

BATIAN

S.W. RIDGE

BROCHEREL COULOIR

TO KRAPF GL.

90

KEY

A. AMPHITHEATRE
B. BAILLIE'S BIV.
D. DE GRAAF'S VARN.
L. LEDGES
M. MACKINDER'S CHIMNEY
M.G. MACKINDER'S GENDARME
O. ONE O'CLOCK GULLY

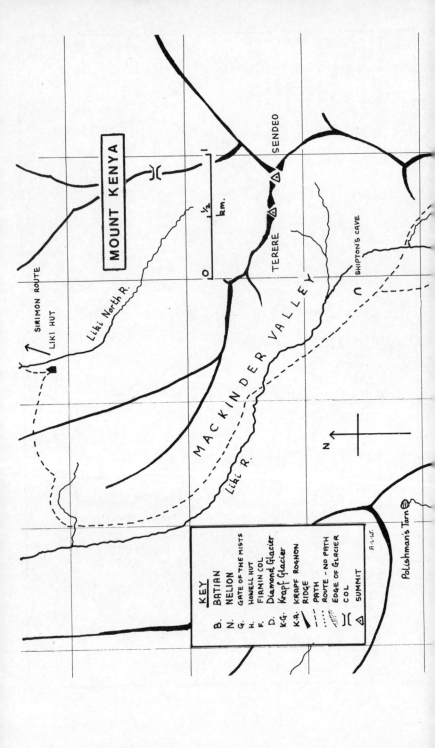

MOUNT KENYA

SIRIMON ROUTE
LIKI HUT
Liki North R.

MACKINDER VALLEY

Liki R.

N

SENDEO

TERERE

SHIPTON'S CAVE

Polishman's Tarn

A.L.W.

KEY
B.   BATIAN
N.   NELION
G.   GATE OF THE MISTS
H.   HOWELL HUT
F.   FIRMIN COL
D.   Diamond Glacier
K.G. Krapf Glacier
K.R. KRAPF ROGNON
      RIDGE
------ PATH
------ ROUTE - NO PATH
      EDGE OF GLACIER
)(COL
△   SUMMIT

½ km.

0

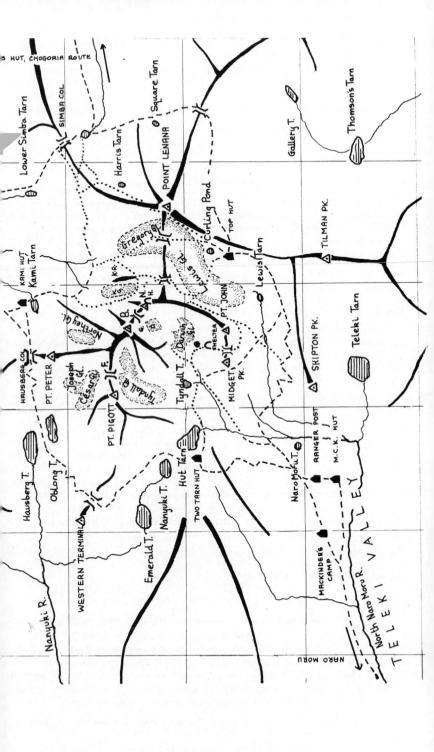

c) The Old Moses route follows the ridges N of the Naro Moru stream and provides some of the most beautiful forest walking and scenery on the mountain. From a road head at c.2800m. game trails lead past good campsites to a picturesque stream crossing and magnificent heather forests. Beyond, a ridge is followed to the moorland; good caves at c.3500m. At c.4150m. an easy traverse leads into the Teleki Valley (6 h. from roadhead), or Two Tarn Hut can be reached in an extra hour up the ridge.

Elephant and buffalo are frequently met along these 3 trails.

ROUND THE PEAKS WALK

A well cairned tour giving magnificent views of the peaks.

Two Tarn Hut to Kami Hut. From the hut go NW, past the second tarn (Nanyuki). Drop slightly, then traverse between 2 cliff bands and ascend scree to a col just R of the Western Terminal. Descend the other side to Oblong and Hausberg tarns, an unspoilt area suitable for camping. Continue E over boulders then scree to Hausberg Col (4591m.). Kami Hut lies a short way below this col; trend R (3 h.).

Kami Hut to Top Hut. Losing no height, traverse SE across steep scree, then among rocky bluffs, to reach Simba Col (4620m.). Descend to Simba Tarn, then go S along a gently rising path, past Square Tarn to a col in a jagged ridge. Traverse W till the ridge just below Top Hut is reached (3½ h.).
   Variations: (a) From Kami Hut, before the rocky bluffs, move higher (SE) and reach Harris Tarn (4725m.). From here scramble up the N ridge of Lenana, turning a gendarme R just below the summit. A very sporting route; rope useful and an ice axe is necessary from mid-December to end March when the ridge is snow covered. Descend the easy S ridge to Top Hut. (b) Along the scree traverse from Kami hut, then climb steep scree on W side of the Gregory Glacier, moving onto the glacier to gain the col (4873m.) leading to the Lewis Glacier. Go down this, keeping L (E) to Top Hut.

From Top Hut follow down the tourist path towards the Teleki Valley. Coming down Lewis Tarn can be seen below and R at the snout of the Lewis Glacier. A stream issues from this and shortly plunges over a rockband; below, it flows across a flat area before dropping down a steep slope. Leave the path and aim for the flat area. Cross it then follow a cairned route NW, traversing below Midget Peak to reach the crest of terminal moraine below the Tyndall Glacier. A gently rising traverse W with some scrambling leads to Hut Tarn and Two Tarn Hut (4490m.) (2¼ h.). Going the other way round the walk to Top Hut would be 1 h. longer.

CLIMBS ON BATIAN AND NELION

90 Normal Route (SE Side)   300m.   IV ***   5 h. to Nelion.

E.E.Shipton, P.Wyn Harris, 1929. Most of the climbing is I/II, with pitches of III+/IV- and one of IV. The Howell biv. hut sits on top of Nelion. The higher (by 11m.) Batian summit stands 150m. away across the 45m. deep gap called Gate of the Mists (5144m.). This section, there and back, takes 3 h. with rocks of III+ and steep snow (axe useful). All pegs are in place. In descent, attention must be paid to route finding; many old slings litter the rocks. Season: late December to mid-March. At other times the route is snowy and possibly icy on the crux.

From Top Hut cross the Lewis gl. horizontally; crampons not essential. On the far side climb steep bouldery scree to foot of cliffs some 50m. L of an icy L-facing couloir.

Easy rocks for 20m. to a big terrace. Move L to a gully, snow possible. Ascend this for 20m., then traverse a long way R on easy ledges. Continue traversing R, round a corner (III-) to base of a deep, long chimney (Mackinder's). Go down 2m. then 6m. R to platform with peg belays. At R end of ledge, step round an edge to a crack in a steep wall. Climb this (IV-) then wider cracks to a big ledge (20m.). On the R is the base of One O'Clock Gully. Follow this for 10m. then step round an arête to R, climb down the other side of it and follow easy narrow ledges till a steep, easy chimney (4m.) leads to broad scree covered ledges crossing the slabby face. Halfway across these climb ledges and slabs to steeper easy rocks, trending slightly R to reach Baillie's Biv., about 60m. above the broad scree covered ledges, and 3m. below the ridge crest. Above, the ridge steepens to a wall leading to the top of Mackinder's Gendarme. Baillie's Biv. is normally ice-filled and very cramped. (It is possible to reach this spot by continuing higher up One O'Clock Gully before traversing R).

Cross over the ridge, go down and L for 10m. then up easy rocks L of gendarme, aiming for a long L-facing corner line; the base of this is reached over a few steeper steps. Above is the crux, De Graaf's Variation. Climb the square cut corner direct to a ledge (20m., IV). Now easier climbing (25m.) to R end of a wide ledge below a sheer, vertical wall. Traverse R and down, crossing the steep upper rocks of an amphitheatre (III+) to gain the other side, then ascend to easier ground in a gully. Follow this over a steepening (III-) to the upper easy section. Near the gully top steep, easy rocks on R lead to the Nelion summit. Scramble along ridge and abseil into Gate of the Mists. (Possible to leave a 45m. rope hanging into the gap and across to the other side, to facilitate the return). Traverse the R (N) side below a gendarme and move up to a ridge. Now traverse horizontally L on S face of Batian, to reach ledges and an ice filled chimney. Climb walls R of this (III+) to easier ground and the summit. In reverse, to avoid the III+ pitch, abseil down the ice filled chimney. From the Gate of the Mists climb snow slopes on L to regain the ridge.

Descent: From Nelion scramble S to locate the easy descent gully. Some 50m. down this, ledges lead off R. From these abseil S down the sheer vertical wall - noted above - to regain the wide ledge. At its E end abseil to the top of De Graaf's. From here a long abseil to easy rock just below Mackinder's Gendarme. Abseil or climb down from Baillie's Biv. and reach the wide scree covered ledges. Traverse these S-wards; at their end move down L of wall and down the steep easy 4m. chimney. Continue traversing until One O'Clock Gully is reached. From the ledge below this, 2 long abseils land at the bottom.

South Face

The best conditions for snow/ice climbs here occur between mid-May and late October. Good snow is still possible at Christmas, following the short rains. After mid January conditions are likely to be poor. The climbs are reached from the foot of the Darwin gl. (E side). The best base is either a boulder shelter 10 min. walk from the foot of the gl., or Two Tarn Hut; from the latter follow the long traverse route to the Tyndall gl. moraine, then gain the base of the Darwin gl. ($1\frac{1}{2}$ h.).

91 Ice Window Route 400m. 3/4 *** 7 h. to Gate of the Mists.

P.Snyder, Y.Laulan, S.LeDain, 1973. A fine ice climb with an unusual and spectacular series of moves to gain the Diamond Glacier below the Gate of the Mists. The middle section takes a narrow ice gully just R of the Diamond Couloir. A few

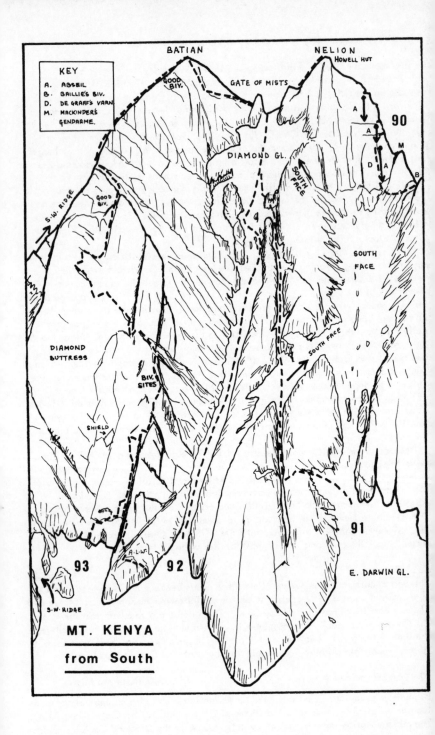

KEY
A. ABSEIL
B. BAILLIE'S BIV.
D. DE GRAAF'S VARN
M. MACKINDER'S GENDARME.

BATIAN

NELION

Howell Hut

GOOD BIV.

GATE OF MISTS

90

A

A

D   A

M

B

DIAMOND GL.

SOUTH FACE

S.W. RIDGE

GOOD BIV

SOUTH FACE

SOUTH FACE

DIAMOND BUTTRESS

BIV. SITES

SHIELD

91

93

92

A.L.W.

E. DARWIN GL.

S.W. RIDGE

MT. KENYA

from South

ice screws and rock pegs are useful.

Start at base of an icefall at top of the E half of the Darwin gl. From here make a long diagonal traverse L, steep and exposed, to the buttress crest and a good belay. Step down and traverse L with difficulty to a long narrow ice gully. Take this (2/3) to a belay on the L. Continue by an easy-angled snowfield up to a continuation of the gully. Shortly the gully steepens and presents a low ice wall. Climb this (3) then the gully above till an exposed ramp leads to the great ice cave below the lip of the Diamond gl. Possible biv. site. Go L down an ice tunnel and swing out (sensational) through an ice window, which may have to be enlarged, to base of the Diamond gl. where it drops vertically for some 50m. to the Diamond Couloir below. Now 4 straightforward pitches lead to Gate of the Mists. In latest season the ice window and cave have been avoided by a long traverse L just below them, leading directly to base of the Diamond gl.

Descend by the Normal Route or South Face Route.

South Face Route 2/3 * The easiest route to Gate of the Mists. Start as for R.91, but traverse R across the snowband at top of the first ice gully. Then go up the easy snowfield and traverse L and upward below the steep walls of Nelion. This leads to a ridge overlooking the Diamond gl. which is reached by a horizontal traverse; then 2 pitches to Gate of the Mists.

92 Diamond Couloir 400m. 5 *** 9 h. to Gate of the Mists.

P.Snyder, T.Mathenge, 1973 (avoiding headwall by ramp on L). By the headwall: Y.Chouinard, M.Covington, 1975. A superb climb; several rock and ice pegs quite useful.

As the first icefall is long it is advisable to climb a short way from the base to belay on the R before tackling the steeper second half. Above follow about 6 easier pitches to a belay slightly R of and above the foot of the great headwall. Move L onto the steep ice and climb it trending L to easier angled ground L of the icefall and an excellent spike. Now 2 ways: A short chimney to the L leads to the Diamond gl., or move R up an ice slope to gain the Ice Window and cave. Either way leads in 4 easier pitches to Gate of the Mists.

S side rock routes on Batian are in best condition from mid-December to mid-March. At other times they are likely to be heavily iced. A great expanse of steep rock, the Diamond Buttress, rises L of the Diamond Couloir. The climbs are excellent but hard to complete in a day. L of the couloir the first major fault is a vertical system of cracks and L-facing corners, marking line of the Original Route. The corner is undercut and access is gained either by starting almost at the foot of the next, less distinct, vertical fault line to the L; or using easy ledges to enter the corner from well to the R. Either way is best reached up the W side of the Darwin gl; 30 min. from boulder shelter at base of the E Darwin gl. or 1½ h. from Two Tarn Hut.

93 Diamond Buttress Original Route 450m. VI *** 15 h.

D.J.Temple, I.F.Howell, 1976. A good selection of nuts is recommended.

L-hand start: Just R of the less distinct fault line. Climb 10m. to a ledge (IV-). An obvious crack for 15m. (IV+). Traverse 10m. R (III) to base of a L-facing long crack, formed by a huge flake. The crack for 30m. (sustained, VI+). Move 8m. R (III) to gain the main fault line.

Var. R-hand start: Scramble L-wards up easy ledges to where the ledges lead back

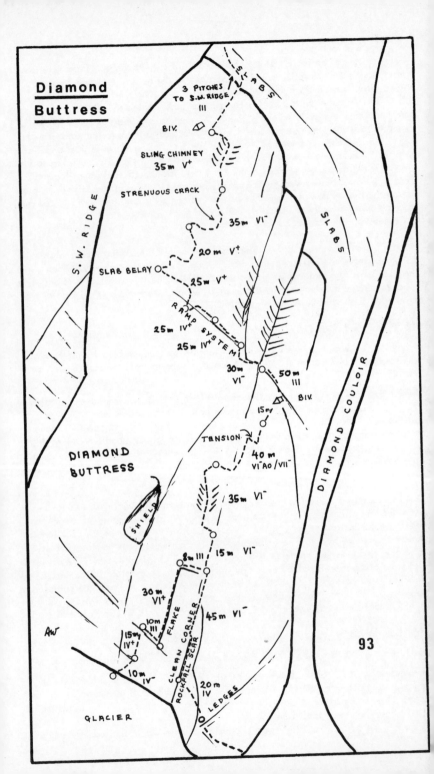

R and upwards towards the Diamond Couloir. Move L for 20m. to a corner (IV). Climb the fine corner, making a delicate traverse into a corner further L and go up this to join the previous start in 45m. (VI-).

Continue with a 15m. pitch (VI-) to a boulder belay where the corner above looks uninviting. Go L and climb a V-chimney; at the top of this move L then R and go up wall to a ledge (35m., VI-). Now move R to a crack and climb this (V+) until the blank R wall can be crossed by a tension traverse (VII-, free) to belay in chimney (40m.). Continue to top of chimney and ledges with good biv. site (15m.). Slant L up slabs to obvious R-facing corner (50m., III).

The buttress is cut at this level by a long ramp/slab system. The next section traverses this L. Move L for 30m. then slightly down to foot of wall; climb this (15m., VI-). Now 2 pitches trending L to a short chimney (25m., 25m., IV+). The chimney then a sloping ramp/slab L to a prominent blank slab (25m., V+). Traverse R across a steep wall, round a nose into a groove, and go up this to a ledge (V+). Traverse R and down to base of a narrow jamming crack; climb this (VI-) to a ledge (35m.). The wall above, turning an overhang by a strenuous move L (35m., V+). Excellent biv. on L. Now 3 easier pitches lead to the SW ridge route; follow this to the summit of Batian.

**South-West Ridge IV+ ** ** A short way L of R.89 low-angled slabs allow a rising traverse L to be made to a notch between a small point (Point Slade) and the SW ridge of Batian proper. On the other side of the notch is an amphitheatre; in snowy conditions quite pleasant, but nasty if icy. In the latter case it is better to follow the ridge above the notch. This terminates in steep walls. A L-ward traverse across the top of the amphitheatre leads to top part of the L bounding ridge of the amphitheatre. At the top of this either go straight up (steep, with small holds) to gain the final sections of the ridge in about 3 pitches; or make a long traverse R, then up a strenuous chimney and corner to gain the upper SW ridge slightly lower down. Then fine climbing to the summit; good biv. site 2 pitches below the top.

94 West Face 450m. 4/5 ** 9 h.

R.A.Caukwell, G.W.Rose, 1955. A fine snow/ice climb L of the SW ridge. It remains in good condition for most of the year, but may lose a lot of cover and become icy from late January to the long rains. A few ice and rock pegs useful.

From Two Tarn Hut traverse to the Tyndall gl. and ascend it to below the final, N-most hanging gl. (1½ h.). Climb steep snow trending R to gain the top of the Heim gl., the lowest hanging gl. at R foot of the face. From the upper slopes climb mixed snow, rock and ice for 3 pitches till long snow/ice ribs on R side of the ice field lead to a slightly steeper pitch, and to a long, horizontal, easy-angled band. Possible biv. in a cave R. From here a long traverse L leads to a gully and hence the summit; or trend R up rock (IV) to reach the SW ridge. Another variant makes a long traverse L across the easy-angled band, then climbs rock to reach the base of a gully leading to the summit; this gully does not merge with the top of the main icefields below.

95 West Ridge 350m. V- * 9 h. from Firmin Col.**

E.E.Shipton, H.W.Tilman, 1930. Bounds L side of the W face, and reputed to be the finest mountaineering route on Mt. Kenya. Awkward access and rarely climbed. Best season, July to October; crampons useful.

Approach is easiest via the Josef gl., reached from just below and W of Hausberg

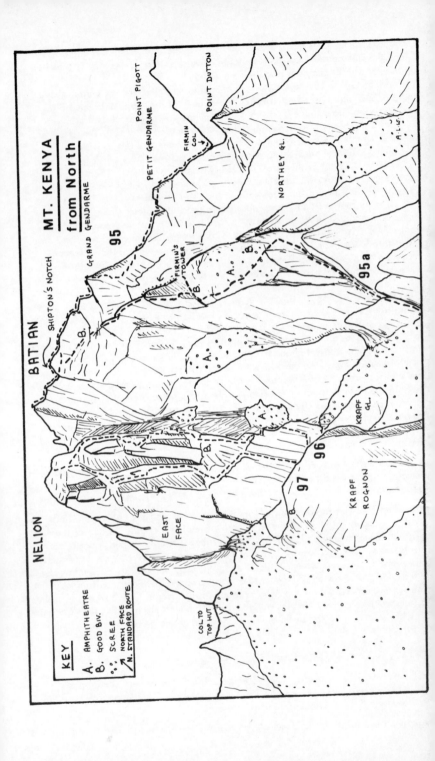

MT. KENYA
from North

KEY

A. AMPHITHEATRE
B. GOOD BIV.
∘∘∘ SCREE
━━ NORTH FACE
╌╌→ N. STANDARD ROUTE

NELION

BATIAN

SHIPTON'S NOTCH

GRAND GENDARME

PETIT GENDARME

Point Pigott

Point Dutton

FIRMIN COL

NORTHEY GL.

95

95a

FIRMIN'S TOWER

B.

B.

A.

A.

B.

A.

EAST FACE

97

96

B.

KRAPF GL.

KRAPF ROGNON

COL TO TOP HUT

Col (4591m.). Halfway up the gl., good biv. ledges on R, about 1½ h. from Kami Hut. Ascend gl. to a 100m. gully of rotten rock or snow (I), hence Firmin Col, c.4850m. (1 h.). An alternative fast approach from Kami Hut involves scrambling up the W side of the Northey gl. to a col between the Petit Gendarme (4976m.) and Pt. Dutton (4885m.), from where the gendarme is reached by easy slabs.

The ridge is climbed over several gendarmes. The Petit Gendarme is mounted slightly S of the crest, traversing onto the N side just before the top. Descend N side to a gap; keep low and L to traverse below the next obstacle, the Grand Gendarme (5099m.). When traversing is no longer possible, difficult slabs are ascended. Then a corner is turned R and a wide ledge is reached. The ridge can now be rejoined behind the gendarme. Follow crest to the "12m. Pinnacle", one of the hardest problems on the route. The next feature is Shipton's Notch; abseil into this, then follow ridge to summit. It is possible to traverse onto N side of the ridge and make a long traverse into the notch.

95a North Face Standard Route   550m.   IV+ **   10 h.

A.H.Firmin, P.Hicks, 1944. The easiest and most popular rock route on Batian between June and October.

Going E from Kami Hut, round the foot of N ridge of Batian, a scree slope is reached leading to the small Krapf gl., lying below the E face of Nelion. The route starts about halfway up this scree slope on the R, at the base of a major couloir system and just above a small biv. site L of a wet chimney.

From a cross-on-circle chipped in the rock, climb up then R into couloir (20m., IV-). Easy rock on L (20m., II). Scramble 45m. up couloir, ignoring branch on L, to narrows; climb these mainly on R (30m., II). The couloir fans out and steepens. Climb a R-facing corner in centre of fan to slabby corner (35m., III+). (Var: cracks and ribs just R of corner lead to ledge on R then a short steep corner to the slabs, 35m., III+). Climb to top L of slabs (35m., I), then a L-facing corner to big terrace (15m., II). Now L up easy gully, back R then take central shallow chimney to ledges at top of the couloir (30m., III+). Scramble up 35m. L to amphitheatre; traverse up and across this to upper L edge; good bivs. on R. Slabs then walls to L skyline ridge just below Firmin's Tower (45m., III). Easily for 10m. to base of tower and good biv. (4 h.). Climb a crack till it divides (20m., IV+). Chimney up R branch for 15m. to great loose block (overlooking the amphitheatre). Move L into the original chimney and continue for 10m. (25m., IV-). Easy steep rock to top of the tower, 5045m. (50m., II). (Var: if there is little snow or ice, it is easier to traverse R beneath the tower and climb icy rocks overlooking the Northey gl. to ridge crest; pegs and slings in place, IV). Now descend to a col, follow ridge for 60m. to a short steep wall, climb this on the R then traverse R to a wide couloir (30m., IV-). Scramble up this to W ridge; at this junction, good biv.). Scramble along scree ledges on N side of ridge then make a short step to reach Shipton's Notch; rotten rock. (Var: the ridge itself can be followed; harder). Continue by ridge for 3 pitches to the summit (II). Descend the same way.

96   East Gate   400m.   V+ ***   10 h.

I.F.Howell, P.Brettell, 1980. An excellent rock climb for the period June to September. Takes walls and corners overlooking the "Supercouloir"; this divides the E face of Nelion from Batian.
Approach as for R.95a and by the Krapf gl., to start some 30m. L of lowest point of

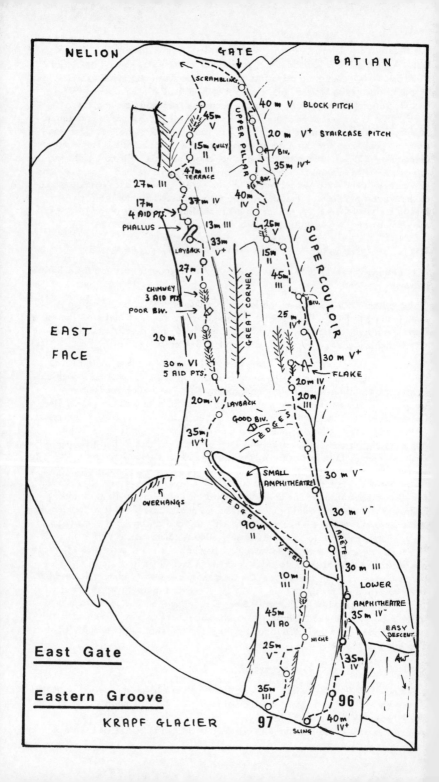

Nelion E face, where a rising traverse line R leads onto the face. Follow this, then move up and R again to reach a slab (IV+) with difficulty (40m.). Avoid a chimney by moving R and ascend to ledges overlooking the amphitheatre low down in Supercouloir (35m., IV). Take ledges on L side of amphitheatre to where easy ledges return L to ridge bounding the L side of Supercouloir (35m., IV-). Ledges L and a short chimney to gain the crest (30m., III). In 5m. two ways are possible. (a) An easy ramp/ledge system L for 60m. to a small scree-filled amphitheatre. Then 40m. up and R to an excellent biv. ledge. This lies just below the huge, open-book corner in the middle of the E face at c.4900m. (b) By the ridge, an awkward chimney then a groove on L in 2 pitches (30m., 30m., V-)

Note: From the biv. ledge a short easy pitch leads to foot of the open-book corner; this is taken by the Scott-Braithwaite Route and provides some of the best climbing on the E face.

East Gate continues from the R-hand end of biv. ledge. Scramble to base of the R-most of 2 corners above (20m., III). The corner, to belay on the R, above a roof (20m., IV). Move down and R across a slab below a roof, to reach a flake. Descend round this to a ledge, then climb grooves on R (30m., V+). Follow the groove line (IV+) to big ledge and possible biv. site (25m.). From far L end of ledge climb a groove (III) then easier rocks to ledges leading L (45m.). Follow these to base of a short steep corner (15m., II). The corner (V, old peg), then a good belay ledge 7m. higher (25m.). Ascend to slab below roof. Move R then L to short chimney. Above this move up and R to a good ledge; possible biv., no water (40m., IV). This point is just below a huge featureless pillar; above that are easy rocks to the summit.

From ledge, climb to and work R across a dirty, wet ledge. Take awkward cracks to a tiny biv. site (with water) at base of a smooth wall (35m., IV+). The wall is split by a fine crack. R of this is a more broken crack system, with ledges resembling a staircase. Climb the Staircase pitch (V+) to a sloping ledge and spike belay (20m.). Gain the top of a flake and move R across it. Make a long step R to reach a short corner. Climb this (V) then ledges and corners to easy ground (40m.). A short scramble trending L leads to Nelion summit.

97 Eastern Groove VI+/A1, or VII- *** 16 h.

I.F.Howell, I.J.Allan, 1978. Another excellent route. On the 3rd ascent all aid was eliminated and the move L to the phallic rock was avoided by climbing more or less direct (E.Hart, M.Christensen, M.Hafner, 1979).

Start 25m. L of East Gate and just L of a smooth slab. Climb R across easy slabs and ledges to easy grooves. These lead to a niche with an overhung R wall (35m., III). Exit L onto slabs and ascend these trending slightly R to swing R, round an edge, and up 6m. to a niche (25m., V-). Move up to a vertical crack, climb this (VI, one aid point) and continue up a ramp sloping L (possible belay); halfway up this make an awkward mantelshelf R (VI) to reach bottom of an off-width crack. Ascend this (one aid point) to belay (45m.). Easier ground to a large shelf (10m., III).

Go L along shelf for nearly 90m., to a point some 15m. from its L end. The Groove itself can be seen above and slightly R of this point as a shallow, square-cut dièdre forming the next main feature L of huge corner in centre of the E face. 2 pitches lead to its base; first curve R-wards on doubtful rock (35m., IV+), then follow a layback crack, step L to a groove and go up to belay at foot of the Groove (20m., V). (If the biv. at c.4900m. below the great corner is used, the Groove can be reached by a simple scramble from L end of the shelf. The bottom

of the layback crack is then best reached by 2 easy, short pitches; the first to ●
terrace below the giant corner, the next traversing slightly down and across to the
layback).

At first the groove is blank and needs some 5 points of aid (wires) until it relents
to jamming and bridging (30m., VI). Continue by cracks to easier ground and a
poor biv. site (20m., VI). 2 more pitches each with occasional aid points lead to c
belay at foot of a layback crack. Climb this (V+) and move L to a phallic rock
(30m.). Slabs behind (III) lead to a vertical corner crack; avoid this by an off-
width crack round a corner L (15m.); some aid points in this crack; then move back
R to easier ground (20m.). 2 easier pitches (40m., IV & 25m., III) attain a large
terrace. Follow this R for 45m. to a scree gully (III). The gully to base of a chimney on the R (15m., II). The chimney (V) to easier ground (45m.) and a short
scramble to Nelion summit.

OTHER CLIMBS

98 Point John Couloir 120m. 3 ** 2-3 h.

P.Snyder, D.Karinga, T.Mathenge, S.Gitonga, 1972. A pleasant ice climb aff-
ording 3 ice and 3 snow pitches. The start is 10 min. walk from boulder shelter
below the E Darwin gl., under the obvious couloir N of Point John. Facing N,
the couloir is in best condition between December and March. At other times the
snow/ice may vanish. Descent: from col at top (c.4800m.), a descending traverse
NE (towards Pt. Lenana) leads to an easy scree gully. The boulder shelter can be
regained by traversing below Pt. John, then crossing the col (4649m.) between Pt.
John and Midget Peak.

99 Point John South Ridge 200m. IV- ** 4 h.

R.Merendi, L.Marimonti, G.Gualco, 1958. Pleasant and exposed rock climb,
easily reached from most locations on this side of the peak. The great vertical
walls of Pt. John become more broken on the R and are terminated by the SE gully,
a wide, slabby couloir, partly scree-filled. Start at gully base. Traverse L then
go up to a white spot on the S ridge. Climb steep rock to a little gully, and take
the R branch of this to top of first tower. The second tower is climbed from L to R.
2 more towers lead to top, just R of the summit tooth (4883m.).
Descend by scrambling towards the head of the SE gully and enter this by a short
abseil, then easy scrambling to the bottom.

Point Peter (4757m.). From Kami Hut, a pleasant short day by S ridge of Pt.
Peter (III+), starting from a col (c.4690m.). Follow ridge avoiding most difficult-
ies on the R side. Descend by one abseil NE into a gully, then an easy scramble.
The N (Window) ridge is another fine training climb (VI).

From the above col (c.4690m.), Point Dutton (4885m.) can be reached by climbing
the N ridge to top of the N couloir, then the short NW ridge to summit (I), 2 h.

99a Point Dutton East Ridge 250m. IV** 4 h.

From centre of the Kami (NE) face, climb easily L and up for 200m. across ledges,
slabs and short gullies to gain L edge of the face (I). Climb a clean corner (15m.,
III+). A more broken corner (20m., III) leads to easy rock, ledges then scree
overlooking the Northey gl. Go up these L then R to a gully leading towards NE

summit. Climb gully for 10m. then go R and up to ridge below a prominent rocky finger (30m., III). Climb a dièdre just L of this (peg at crux), move L and take slabs to a flake (25m., IV+). Now the ridge to NE summit (45m., IV–). So follow sharp crest for 150m. to final wall (pass R) and the main summit.

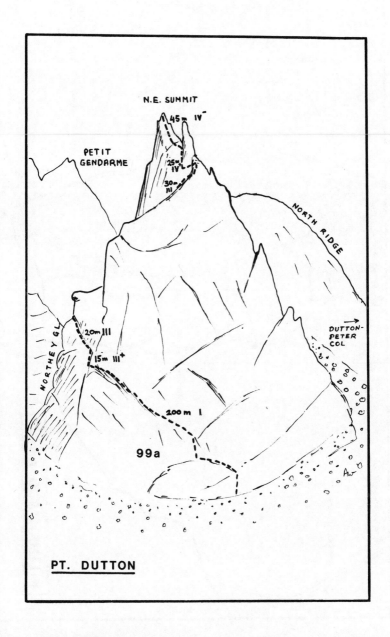

PT. DUTTON

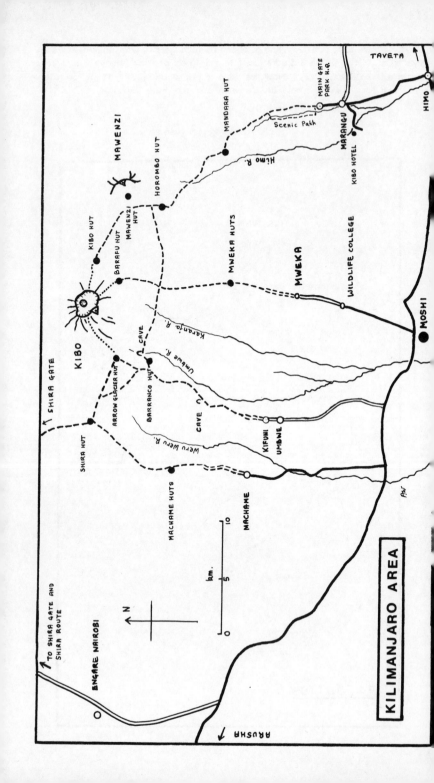

KILIMANJARO

KILIMANJARO (5896m.), the highest mountain in Africa, has less to offer the climber than Mt. Kenya. However, some of the climbs are outstanding and the Umbwe route followed by the Heim Glacier is one of the world's great mountaineering expeditions. Uhuru Peak is the highest point on Kibo, the main pudding-shaped elevation. Mawenzi (5149m.) is just lower than Mt. Kenya, more jagged and separated from Kibo by The Saddle, a flat semi-desert area extending for 5 km. Both mountains have poor rock. The majestic SW face of Kibo is steep and heavily glaciated, extending for 5 km. and broken only by one easy passage - The Western Breach. The well equipped Marangu route from the E supplies the easiest approach. Beautiful forests and moorlands are followed by the Saddle; finally tedious scree leads to the Kibo crater and Uhuru Peak. The SW side of Kibo is best reached by the remote and demanding Umbwe or Machame routes - only suitable for experienced mountaineers. The high level Kibo South Circuit links the remote SW areas with the Marangu route and provides magnificent views of the ice-cliffs.

Kilimanjaro National Park is well organized but very expensive. The average visitor for 5 days pays about $250 (in foreign exchange) before entry. This covers park fees and a mandatory guide. Only at the main Marangu gate can fees be paid, and porters and guides obtained. Beware of pilfering by unsupervised porters.

As on Mt. Kenya it is important to acclimatize well to enjoy the ascent of Kibo. Routes start at less than 2000m. and it is recommended that at least 3 days are taken to reach the final cone. The weather on Kilimanjaro, though generally drier, follows a similar pattern to that on Mt. Kenya. The SW glaciers have their winter season between May and late October. Snow cover is then at its best though it is often misty. The best weather is between January and March but usually by mid-February the glaciers are becoming very icy and devoid of snow.

The Kibo Hotel in Marangu (PO Box 102, Marangu, Kilimanjaro, tel. Marangu 4) is well-run, hires equipment (limited selection) and arranges porters and guides. The Park offers similar facilities; contact The Warden, Kilimanjaro National Park, PO Box 96 Marangu, tel. Marangu 50. The YMCA at Moshi is a more convenient base for the Umbwe and Machame routes.

Food, petrol and many other basics are scarce in Tanzania. Tanzanians often obtain supplies in Kenya and the Kenyan Shilling is thus highly valued by them (black market rates are 5:1 as opposed to the official rate of 1:1). Unofficial dealings in Kenyan and Tanzanian currencies are illegal, and bank notes should not be taken out of their countries of origin. A car brought into Tanzania requires road tax, valid for 3 months, and costs 1000 TSh; or 1000 KSh can be tendered. Namanga is the most convenient crossing point from Kenya.

ACCESS

(i) Tarmac roads to the Marangu park gates. Nairobi to Namanga, 170 km; Namanga to Arusha, 110 km; Arusha to Moshi, 90 km; Moshi to Himo, 27 km; Himo to Kibo Hotel, 11 km; Kibo Hotel to Marangu Gate, 8 km.

(ii) For Umbwe take the Moshi-Arusha road; 2 km. from Moshi dirt roads lead to Umbwe in a further 14 km. A dirt track continues for 3 km. to Kifuni. Vehicles without 4 WD will not get far beyond here; the track enters the forest and becomes narrow and steep. For security it may be possible to arrange parking at the Umbwe Mission School.

(iii) For Machame take the Moshi-Arusha road for 9 km. to where a tarmac road leads in 14 km. to Machame village. It is possible to drive, with difficulty, for another 6 km. The park check point is at the edge of the forest.

Buses and matatus go from Nairobi to Namanga and on to Moshi regularly. From there, Marangu, Machame and Umbwe are all served by buses, matatus and taxi. Kilimanjaro International Airport lies just off the Moshi-Arusha road, 34 km. from Moshi.

WALKING ROUTES

1. Normal Route

From the Marangu Gate (1980m.) a wide path leads through forest to the Mandara Hut at 2700m. (4 h.). A path further. W, starting just beyond the park gate, is 30 min. longer but passes through some of the most beautiful forest hereabouts. In descent the start is clearly marked, about 1 h. below Mandara.

Shortly after leaving the Mandara Hut the forest gives way to giant heather, and then moorland; the roomy Horombo huts are situated in this zone at 3700m. (5 h.). Not far beyond these huts a faint but well marked trail traverses off L to the Barranco Hut; a long day's walk. On our route, higher up the vegetation thins and the last water/stream is passed. The path continues to the gravelly Saddle which is crossed at length to the Kibo Huts, situated just below the scree slopes of Kibo at 4700m. (5 h.). If there is little snow, water may have to be carried up to here.

Starting well before dawn, climb the tedious scree to the crater rim and Gillman's Point (5680m.) (5 h.). For this achievement a certificate is given at the park gate. Now more easily along the crater rim for about $1\frac{1}{2}$ km. to Uhuru Peak (5896m.) ($1-1\frac{1}{2}$ h.).

In descent each leg can be done comfortably in 3 h. The huts on this route are very comfortable and camping is no cheaper. All of them have radios.

2. Umbwe Route

On this and the next routes water is very scarce. Carry an adequate supply, as dehydration accentuates altitude sickness. From Kifuni (1500m.) an old vehicle track continues about 7 km. in forest (3 h.). A marked path turns L off this and in 3 km. a stream and possible campsite are reached (2 h.). Now steeply through forest with glimpses of Kibo or the gorge below. At 2940m. overhangs are reached, good shelters. Water is available in a slow moving stream about 50m. below (3 h.). Soon the forest ends and the path proceeds along a spectacular narrow ridge. At 3500m. a cave (water 10 min. away) could be used as a shelter, but it is better to continue to the Barranco Hut at 3900m. This is beautifully situated at the upper limit of the heather zone and commands superb views of the southern ice cliffs and the Breach Wall; water nearby (5 h.). 30 min. E of hut, following the Kibo South Circuit to the Horombo huts, a stream is crossed before climbing steeply up the side wall of the valley; there is a fine biv. boulder here with firewood nearby.

The Arrow Glacier Hut (4800m.), situated at the foot of the Western Breach, is reached from here by a path which follows the main ridge (500m. W of the hut) and runs N then NW towards the hut site; stream close by (4 h.).

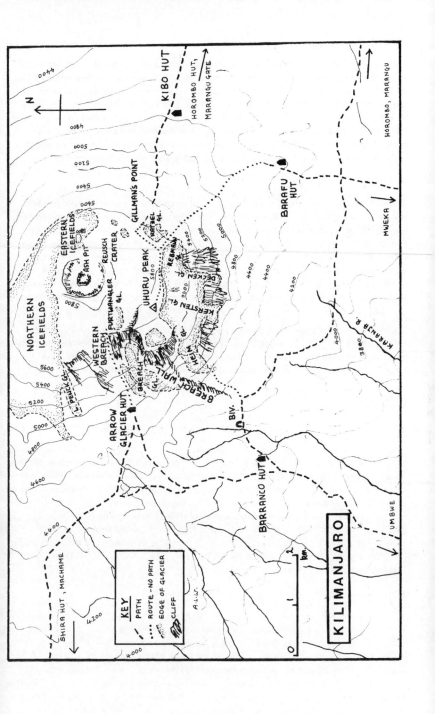

KILIMANJARO

3. Machame Route

From the Park Post (1900m.) a well marked path rises fairly steeply through forest. At 3000m. the forest thins and the Machame huts are reached; stream nearby (5 h.). Above, cross a small valley and continue up ridges and through heather with occasional rock scrambles for about 4 h. to the head of a river valley. Traverse W across this then continue N to the Shira Hut (3800m.); water and firewood close by (5 h.). The Arrow Glacier Hut (4800m.) can be reached by a well-cairned trail, first E then ESE (5 h.); the last section is a steep scree ridge below which a well-marked path (the Kibo South Circuit) leads off R to the Barranco Hut.

4. Kibo South Circuit

A fine traverse. The middle sections provide magnificent views of the ice cliffs above. From Shira Hut to Barranco Hut as noted above (4 h.). Now E to the biv. boulder 30 min. from the Barranco Hut (see Umbwe Route above). Scramble up the steep trail to top of the Breach Wall. (Turn off N at this point for the Heim Glacier). The path now traverses over scree and ridges and drops into the Karanga Valley to a fine campsite and stream ($3\frac{1}{2}$ h.). Climb out of valley and continue traversing tediously over ridges till the Mweka–Barafu hut path is crossed (2 h.). Then traversing again to join the Marangu route just above the Horombo Hut (3 h.).

Mweka Route: This approach to the mountain is not particularly scenic and the first sections are heavily overgrown. From roadhead at Mweka, the Mweka Huts at 3100m. are reached in 5 h., water nearby. The Barafu Huts (4600m.) are 5 h. ahead; the Kibo South Circuit is crossed halfway up. No water en route.

CLIMBS

100 The Western Breach 1100m. I ** 6 h. to summit.

The easiest way on the SW side of the mountain; well marked. The first section is on steep scree above the Arrow Glacier Hut; occasional snow/ice patches. Higher up a pleasant scramble and a short loose section lead to the crater rim, 200m. below Uhuru Peak. In descent route finding may be difficult because the breach fills with clouds in the afternoon. For the summit, 2 ways to continue.
   (i) Traverse 2 km. E then SE across the relatively flat crater floor to attain the Marangu route halfway between Gillman's Point and Uhuru Peak.
   (ii) The Furtwangler Glacier to the SE is skirted either on its R or on its easier N side; beyond, an easy gully leads to the level rim, 100m. W of Uhuru Peak. Ice axe and possibly crampons are useful.

101 Heim Glacier 1200m. 2/3 *** 10 h.

A. Nelson, H.J. Cooke, D.N. Goodall, 1957. The obvious glacier with a dog-leg R of the Breach Wall precipices. An outstanding route; technical difficulties are short. From the Barranco Hut follow the South Kibo Circuit (cutoff point as noted above) and take a rocky then moraine ridge N, directly to foot of glacier. A biv. boulder is situated about 100m. below the glacier snout at 4500m. (3 h.).
   Climb the snout or go up scree on L and traverse onto glacier higher up. Follow the easiest line upwards. The top of Window Buttress can be reached in two ways:
(i) 100m. from its highest rocks, make a traverse L on to a broad ledge on the buttress; follow this L then R to a ramp which is climbed to an ice pitch and the

top (2/3). (ii) The broad ledge can be avoided by climbing 45° ice L-wards to the top in 3 pitches (3) (4 h.). This is the knee of the dog-leg (4800m.). Good biv. site in magnificent surroundings. (From here a long rising traverse L gains the base of the 2 famous Breach Wall icicles, 80m. high).

Climb easy slopes to a steepening taken direct or avoided by gullies well to the L. Beyond the angle relents (biv. sites possible) and the summit ice cliffs can be seen. Aim for the L edge of these and pass below them to reach Uhuru Peak (6 h.).

The 2 icicles mentioned above are part of the Breach Wall Direct Route; the L one was climbed by R.Messner, K.Renzler, 1978 at grade 6. R of the Heim Glacier are 2 other major glaciers, the Kersten and the Decken. It is possible to find a way up the R side of the Kersten at about grade 3/4. The Decken gl. can be climbed at 3. Numerous harder variations exist on all the glaciers.

102 Barafu Route 1300m. I * 6 h.

Combined with the Machame or Umbwe approaches, this adventurous easy itinerary allows the scenery of the Kibo South Circuit to be sampled whilst gaining acclimatization. The Barafu Hut (for access, see Kibo South Circuit above) is situated in a desolate spot. Unless the snowline is low, water can be hard to find. From the hut the W ridge of the SE valley depression is followed. The lip of the crater is reached between the Ratzel and Rebmann glaciers. Uhuru Peak is less than 1 h. away. The final slopes before the lip are steep and can be icy. To avoid cutting steps, crampons could then be useful. In descent, times can be halved.

The Crater and Summit Icefields

For those well acclimatized a bivouac on the crater floor is very much worth the effort as it allows the Northern and Eastern icefields to be explored (outstandingly beautiful at dawn) as well as the inner (Reusch) crater. Inside the latter there are numerous fumaroles and extensive sulphur deposits. The scene within the central Ash Pit is impressive.

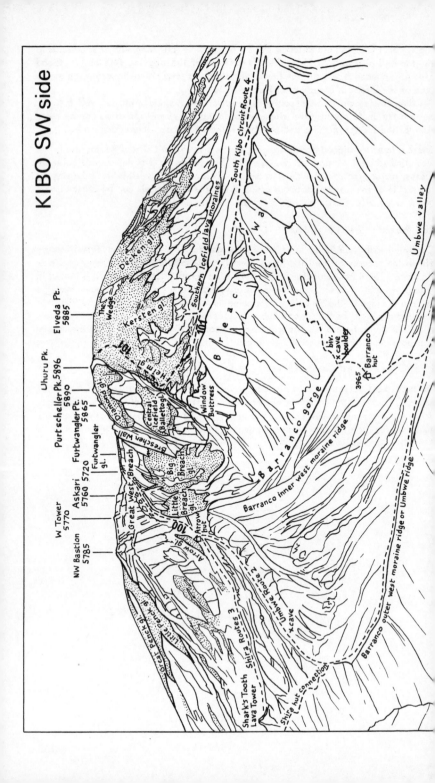

KIBO SW side

SECONDARY AREAS

Nzaui

General: This peak, just under 2000m. high, can be seen clearly from the main Nairobi to Mombasa road on the L-hand side. The cliffs are 300m. high and stretch for well over one km. At the S end they form a nose. The climb described goes up slabs L of the nose to a large vegetated terrace, then takes the exposed nose proper to the summit. Here superb views extend across the plains and Kibo can be seen on clear days. The whole summit area is covered with fine mature pine forest managed by the Forest Department through whom a guest house near the summit (intermittant water supply) may also be booked. It is also possible to camp on the summit or near the guest house with no prior permission. For driving to the guest house or the summit a 4 WD vehicle is essential. Though the climb itself is not outstanding it has a unique atmosphere, and coupled with the drive it makes a first class expedition. The nearest garage facilities, water and petrol are at Emali (47 km.).

Access: The main Mombasa road from Nairobi is taken to Emali. Here turn L and drive along a good dirt road going NE. After 15 km. a village with a roadside market is passed (Matiliku); in another 14 km. a watercourse is crossed; 700m. beyond this, on R-hand side of the road, take a sharp turn R onto a small track signposted "Kyenza Highway". If you miss this turn off, then in exactly 1.6 km. the centre of Nziu village is reached. From the turn off continue along the track for 11 km. to a fork. The L branch goes to the guest house; the R continues for a short distance to the summit. Allow at least 4 h. from Nairobi. Matatus go only as far as the start of the Kyenza Highway.

103 <u>The Nose of Nzaui</u>   V-   250m. ***

.F.Howell, I.J.Allan, 1973. The climb is best reached by abseil from the summit. Scramble down the nose to an easy slab. A short piece of rope attached to the lowest tree can provide an abseil point at the start of a vertical drop. A long abseil from the bottom of the easy slab lands on a vegetated terrace. Walk 50m. S, turn R and go down to the lowest tree above an overhanging wall which allows a long abseil to be made to the slabs below. 2 more long abseils bearing slightly N lead to bottom. Equipment left in place for abseiling might hopefully be retrieved on the way up.
   The bottom can be reached by a less pleasant gully S of the vegetated terrace, followed by a long traverse along foot of the cliff. Continue N below a prominent great red overhang and after a grassy bay the foot of the slabs is reached.

An easy slab near tree, then a short bulge to a wide grassy terrace. The slabs proper start above here (30m.). A hard move is made off the ground up a short steep wall to gain a ledge by a difficult step R. Move across ledge R-wards to a small tree; now climb straight up past a small ledge to excellent gargoyle belays on the wall above; semi-hanging stance (40m.). Either traverse steeply down and R, or go down to a tiny ledge and hence gain a sweep of undulating slabs to R. Go up these, first trending R, then L. Finally move L and up to tiny trees on a ledge system above; a totally unprotected pitch (45m., IV). Aim diagonally R to gain a tree belay below an overhanging red wall (40m.).

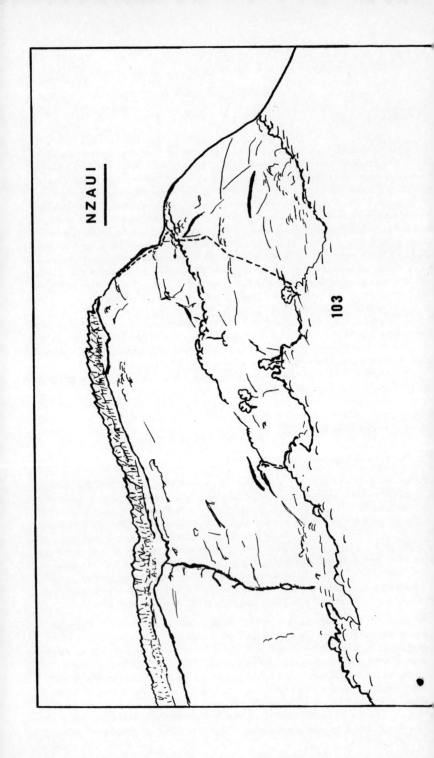

NZAUI

103

Traverse L then gain with difficulty a higher slab level. Climb to a tiny corner just L of the overhanging wall, at the top of the slab. Take corner to finish awkwardly on grass L (40m.).

A scramble follows to the vegetated final step on the nose. Climb a L-trending line of weakness, then straight up to reach 2 bolt belays; do not trend R on any part of this pitch (30m.). Now go up diagonally R over a very steep wall to easy slab finish (25m.).

Hardly any equipment need be carried on this climb as there is little opportunity to use it. Pegs are of no assistance.

o o o o o

Kalama Hill

General: Located in the Machakos District - a high and fertile area inhabited by friendly, industrious people, the Wakamba. Among numerous crags on the sides of this hill, and smaller ones on a facing hill, the biggest are Nzauni and Kiandili; both give routes of 200m. The rock is good quality gneiss, similar to Lukenya, but there are few crack lines and belays are scarce. Access is simple and takes 30 min. on foot. At c.1830m. the altitude ensures that temperatures rarely become oppressive. No good camping in the vicinity; the nearest petrol/garage is at Machakos (33 km.). Water could be obtained at the nearby village of Kali.

Access: From Nairobi follow the main Mombasa road and 9 km. after Lukenya turn off L to reach Machakos in 19 km. Town centre roundabout with clocktower. Turn R here and follow tarmac for 9 km. to a road forking R; ignore this. Bear L on the main road, straight down a hill. In another 12 km. turn R at several small dukas and a hotel with a large Brooke Bond sign. The cliffs can now be seen. In 10 km. reach the village of Kali, served by public transport. Now take tracks leading R-wards towards Nzauni, a short distance away. For Kiandili, turn R up a track about 1½ km. before Kali. Kiandili is distinguished by great orange walls in its L half, with a large band of overhangs at mid-height (no climbs are described here).

NZAUNI

The cliff is divided by a vegetated gully (possible descent route). The R half is slabby with a long overhang at its L end. The L half is steeper with overhanging walls near the top. The central part of the L-hand cliff is ascended by the next 2 routes.

104 <u>Lord of the Flies</u>   V+   185m.   **

M. Harris, R. Chambers, C. Powell, 1966. In centre of the crag, at the foot of the main slab, a stack of boulders has ledges on top; these lie directly below the apex of the orange, arrow-shaped area of overhanging walls above the slabs.

From the R side of the ledges traverse R across a steep wall to gain a steep, bollard-covered slab. Ascend this to a semi-hanging belay on a collection of bollards, just R of a vegetated area (40m.). Now slightly R to avoid vegetation, then move up with difficulty to easier-angled slabs. Belay at base of a L-facing corner on R (45m.). The slab L of corner, to attain ledge on R above corner; stance and belay at small rock pinnacle (20m.). Go up to traverse L over easy slabs and belay below a corner formed at apex of the slabs. The L wall of this is orange and slightly overhanging (35m.). The corner (1 or 2 aid pegs), then traverse R on slabs to easier ground and tree belay (15 m.). Climb steep tapering slab on L; make a thin move L to easier slabs leading to top (30m.). This pitch is avoidable by traversing 15m. R from the belay to easier ground.

Direct Start: At the lowest point of slab, 20m. R of normal start. Climb a short R-facing flake crack, continue in a general direction of 11 o'clock, very thin at first, then the easier bollard-covered face is reached. A fine pitch (45m., VI-, A.Wielochowski, 1984).

Var. Finish: More pleasant and direct, joining the last pitch of Baygon. From the pinnacle belay, climb direct to steep walls and gain the small tree belay ledge below the last pitch of Baygon; finish up this.

105 Baygon   V-   135m. **

A.Wielochowski, R.Corkhill, 1984. R of R.104, at next vegetated pile of boulders with a tree halfway up it.

Climb the L side of this pile to reach an ivy covered ledge on top, directly below an overhanging prow forming the R end of the arrow-shaped, orange, overhanging wallband. Climb in a 10 o'clock direction to below small roof cracked on L. Move L beyond and continue diagonally L to a weakness in steep bulges above, some 5m. R of an obvious vegetated and overhung ledge. Ascend weakness from L to R (crux, unprotected) to easy slabs just below R end of the prow. Possible belay at base of a R-facing corner; better to traverse L below prow to a good stance and thread belay (45m.). Easy slabs L of the orange overhanging walls to ledge and belays (25m.). More easy slabs to a ledge and small tree reached by climbing the orange walls by their shortest section. Traverse delicately R to gain a higher spectacular hand-traverse R below slight roof-line. From the R end follow up a break to easy ground and the top (40m.).

The R half of Nzauni is climbable almost anywhere. Route finding tricky and belays are scarce.

106 Double First   IV   200m. *

R.D.Metcalfe, D.G.Draper, 1966. On slabs rising to R end of a long overhang. Start near base of the central gully, a few m. above lowest point of the cliff, on a horizontal line used by natives as a path.

Trend slightly L up knobbly wall (25m.). Make an ascending traverse L to a yellow pillar breaking through the lower clumps of grass; climb this on awkwardly sloping holds. Traverse 2m. L to a gap in next grass ledge and belay 3m. higher (35m.). A shallow groove leads to L of obvious tree (30m.), then climb trending R to foot of steep wall between 2 big overhangs; tree belay (30m.). Now make a descending traverse R over slabs and grass to big block beside a tree (20m.).

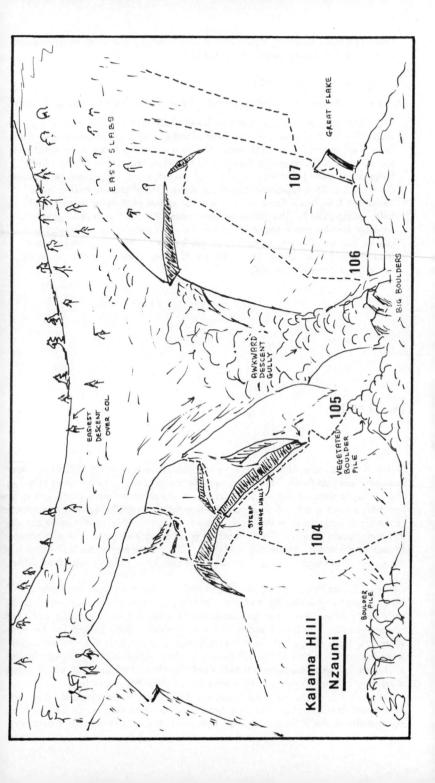

Kalama Hill
Nzauni

EASIEST DESCENT OVER COL

EASY SLABS

GREAT FLAKE

107

106

BIG BOULDERS

AWKWARD DESCENT GULLY

105

VEGETATED BOULDER PILE

STEEP ORANGE WALL

104

BOULDER PILE

Traverse R to an overhung slab. Pull R past overhang and climb to tree belays (20m.). Climb water groove easily (40m.).

107 Flake Route   III+   185m. **

M.Harris, C.Powell, A.McMillan, 1966. Takes slabs just L of centre of the cliff.

Below L edge of an obvious, giant yellowish flake climb smooth slabs to a grassy ledge (20m.). Bridge up behind L edge of flake, step R onto boulders and the flake itself and climb to small trees. Go R up a slanting ledge on face of flake, step up on small holds going slightly L to the edge, and follow this to a large ledge at top (30m.). Move R to centre of the ledge and step up onto wall above. Go up to L until it is possible to move R above tufts of grass towards a large bollard on R skyline. Continue R to a black groove containing several good belay points (45m.). The groove on good holds (20m.). Continue in groove to surmount a bulge and a smoother section above on good holds. Alternative grooves can be climbed, especially on the R (35m.). Now easy angled slabs lead to top (35m.). Direct Var: From top of flake, climb more directly to top, following a water groove (IV).

o o o o o

Soitpus

General: This 200m. high crag is clearly visible on the R from the Nairobi to Mombasa road just past Emali. It faces S and the sound gneiss provides good climbing. The setting is pleasant and wildlife abounds on the plains below the crag and in the beautiful summit woods. Access during wet periods is generally impossible on account of the black cotton soil on the plains around the cliffs; this rapidly becomes very soft and slippery in rain. On the walk up it is best to wear jeans or similar trousers to combat the dense, thorny bush and ticks. Good campsites in the bush at base of the slopes. No water. Garage, etc. at Emali and Sultan Hamud, both about 20 km.

Access: Sultan Hamud is 100 km. from Nairobi on the main Mombasa road. Turn R here. Cross the railway line and turn L onto a pipeline road running parallel to the main road. After 15 km. the road passes over a small hill with watering point and several houses. Turn R here and follow a faint track. Soon Soitpus can be seen. Where the track swings R of the hill turn L and cross an area of black cotton soil. Keep low and skirt base of the hill for about 5 km. before heading straight for the cliff areas. A good campsite lies below and slightly R of a huge block which offers some short climbs. A deep, hidden watercourse splits the ground here.
    The easiest access to the crags is above and slightly R of the campsite, then up to R-hand end of the huge overhangs of the E buttress. From here traverse more or less horizontally to the W buttress routes. Easy grassy descent between the 2 buttresses.

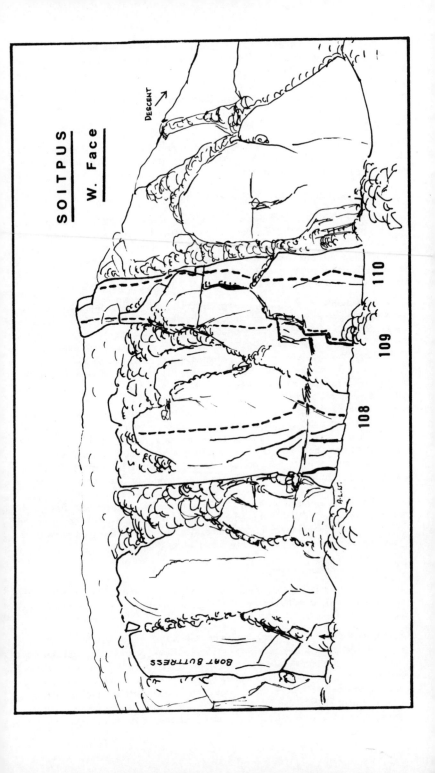

SOITPUS

W. Face

DESCENT

110

109

108

BOAT BUTTRESS

A.L.S.

The climbs described represent only a fraction of all the routes done. Near the L end of the cliffs stands a fine buttress with an overhang low down on its "prow". Boat Buttress (VI- *) gains the crest of the buttress above the overhang by traversing in from the R. Further R the clean buttress in centre of the W face has been climbed by several grade VI routes. R.108 starts near centre of the face.

108 Central Buttress   VI   170m. **

First ascentionists uncertain. A steep awkward wall leads to a R-trending fault. Climb this through bulges to ledges. Move L onto steep slabs. Go up these, poor protection, for 45m. Easier shorter pitches lead to the top.

109 Daphne's Delight   IV   170m. **

W.M.Adams, Miss D.I.Vandepeer. The buttress on the L of the grassy way down, taking highest part of the cliff. For the lower 60m. the buttress has a huge sandy wall at its E end with an enormous ledge and rectangular overhang above at the L. The route goes up to the ledge and traverses L across top part of the overhang to a tree-filled crack leading up towards top of cliff. Start at L end of sandy wall, L of a large tree, on a wall just to R of a large gully leading to the ledge.

> The R-hand arête of the gully; first go up the edge to a smooth black slab overlooking the gully, then move R and up the wall to large flake holds. Climb these to ledge with tree; sustained (35m.). Scramble R through trees and bushes to a chimney; chock belay (30m.). Climb R arête of chimney and enter cavern with large chockstone; behind this, chimney up to large tree belay (15 m.). Ignore easy grass behind, step back down from tree and move L in a wide bridging position to reach a small tree growing out of undercut L wall. Pull up into this tree and follow crack above it. Move L along easy ledges, on top of large rectangular overhang; when holds give out make a move across to a large bushy platform with the aid of a horizontal tree. Go up vegetation to 2 large trees in gully; second crux (30m.). Step up to L-hand arête of gully and follow this on good holds to ledge. Move L then upwards in a superb position, exposed but with enormous holds, to trees on top. An awkward move is necessary to get over the top into the bushes (30m.). Easy scrambling for 60m. leads to a buttress on R. A gully on the L would probably give a scramble to the summit. If you take the R-hand branch, a traverse behind a huge flake gains a good final pitch. From top of huge flake with a deep cleft behind it, mount L up a sloping slab to a smooth arête adorned with hairy patches (lichen); follow this then move L to crack (good runner on L) and so climb to the top (30m.).

110 Gladiator   VI-   160m. **

I.J.Allan, M.Savage, 1976. The R side of buttress climbed by R.109. Start 35m. R of Daphne's Delight and some 6m. R of a groove leading to a tree with grey roots 30m. above the ground.

> A thin start leads to good holds which are followed R-wards for 15m. Then a rising traverse L to a tree in a groove (35m.). Climb groove using roots for 10m., then traverse R along sloping ledge to a thin crack; climb this and walls above to tree (30m.). Traverse 6m. L and go up to tree at foot of steep crack; take this and at end step L to blocks, then L again round lichen arête, moving up to a wide diagonal crack rising L. Climb crack and sloping ledges above to terrace (35m.). Ignore a wide gully straight above terrace. Look to buttress on R of the

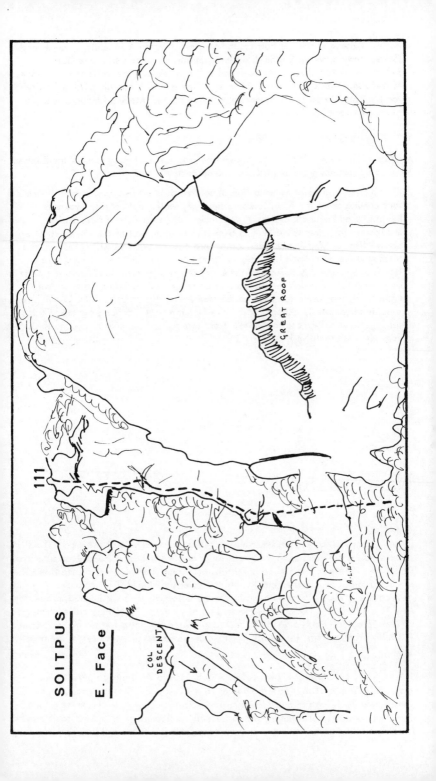

gully. Ascend L arête of buttress for 6m. then traverse R to obvious ear-shaped flake. Now move up L then directly in middle of buttress to a tree (25m.). Behind the belay climb a chock-filled gully for about 15m. to its top at a ledge. A steep thin crack splits the wall on L; climb this with considerable difficulty for 15m. until good holds appear on a lichen bulge. Move up bulge L-wards to grassy terrace (35m.).

111 <u>Spigolo Giallo</u>   V-   100m. **

M.Harris, I.Howell, 1967. The tower-like crag just L of main mass of the E face, reached by scrambling two-thirds way up an approach ramp from L to R.

Go up ramp to a point where a line of weakness (identified by a handrail-like root coming down the face) leads up the steep wall. Follow this weakness keeping L and beneath clumps of vegetation; beyond, ascend more easily straight up for some way until just beneath the steep part of the tower; low tree belay (40m.). Step R round the corner into a broken groove which leads into a V-shaped corner capped by a triangular roof. Ascend to roof; some blocks and flakes need careful handling. At the roof step L with good holds onto the arête and climb this to a slab leading to a large ledge cutting R-hand side of tower (25m.). Ascend arête for a few m. by mantelshelf (or crack on R by jamming) to a point where one is stopped by the overhanging wall. Reach over top of this for jugs, and swing onto the arête. Continue to top, keeping as near to the L edge as possible (35m.).

o o o o o

Kasigau Dome

Driving from Voi to Mombasa the dome may be seen on R side of the road. The cliff is some 300m. high and so far only one route has been accomplished - up a central fault line. There appears to be potential for a long, hard and very steep line to be forced further R in a corner/crack. In the lower half the cliff is composed of bands of featureless slabs with smooth walls above. Although the rock is good, protection is difficult to find. The dome is reached by turning R at a village called Maungu, 30 km. SE of Voi, onto a good dirt road and taking this for a further 30 km. Camping places below cliff which lies 10 min. from the road. Matatus serve the area.

112 <u>Planet Route</u>   VI-   300m. *

I.F.Howell, I.J.Allan, 1974. 100m. of slabs lead to the fault proper. Halfway up slabs, note a long roof with large tree at its R-hand end. 2 pitches reach the tree, the last moves being the crux. Above tree gain the upper slab and make a long L-trending traverse, bolt runner near end. Walk up through trees till the fault can be entered on R. Traverse L below an overhang (bolt just R of crack). Fine chimney

climbing follows.   The final section to the summit is forested.   On the 1st ascent
skulls were found in a cave on the summit.

∘ ∘ ∘ ∘ ∘

Baringo

General: If you have money to spare and enjoy variety in climbing experiences
then a visit to Lake Baringo's Island Camp will certainly be memorable.   The lake
is some 10 km. across and in the centre there is a small island on which this luxury
tented camp is located.   Here is an excellent base for bird-watching, water-skiing,
sailing, sail-boarding, resting and "sea-cliff" climbing on Lesukut.   The latter is
a 400m. long island lying one km. away and providing a variety of short climbs of
40m. maximum on good, clean lava rock in a fine setting.   Some of the routes have
to be reached by boat or by swimming.   Island Camp provides a free boat for climbers, though swimming is a pleasant alternative.   Bookings for Island Camp are made
through Thorn Tree Safaris in Nairobi (PO Box 42475, tel. 25641 or 25941).   During
the week there is generally plenty of room but the camp may be crowded at week-
ends.   The cost for one day's full board for 2 people (in 1984) was 850 KSh for non
residents and 600 KSh for residents.

Access: Good tarmac roads all the way from Nairobi to Lake Baringo (270 km.).
Shortly after passing an airstrip turn R through a small village on the lakeside. From
this a rough track leads in just over one km. to a landing place beside the lake;
here a boat service goes to the island.   Petrol might be available at Lake Baringo
Club but the nearest garages are at Nakuru, 110 km. distant.   Public transport is
available from Nairobi to Nakuru and hence to Lake Baringo.

Access to route nos. 1,2,3 and 4 is from a landing site on L.

1.   VI **   Climb to overhanging roof of cave and over this by a good crack; then
a steep wall to top.

2.   V- *   Climb rotten chimney, traverse L below overhangs, go up zigzag crack
and hence to top.

3.   VI *   Climb a recess to a shallow chimney; go up this to top.

4.   VI+ **   Start at a recessed ledge. Gain slab on L. Move R and climb very
steep crack, moving L at the top (crux) to an easy finish.

Access to routes 4a,b and c is from boulders at water level just R of overhanging
walls.

4a   V- **   From L end of boulders climb a rib, traverse 10m. L under bulging
walls (good protection) then climb a crack to the top.

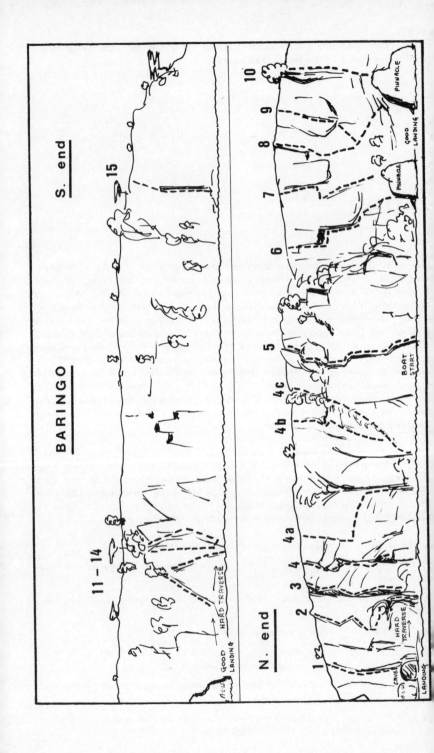

BARINGO

S. end

N. end

Climbing at Baringo.

4b VI-   Climb cracks R-wards to a big bouldery ledge below roofs. Climb over these L then R to easier ground.

4c I An easy descent ramp.

5. IV- **   Reached from a boat. Climb the easy crack which develops into a chimney. Go up this to ledge and tree. The next pitch climbs through overhangs immediately R and above ledge, traversing R below final overhang to finish.

Routes 6 and 7 start from a great rock pinnacle.

6. V+ *   Climb a thin groove, traverse L and climb the great L-facing and over-hanging corner to top. A more difficult approach is directly from the bottom (VI-).

7. VI- **   Take a groove in slab above the pinnacle; above 2 small bushes make a thin traverse R to gain the easier L-facing corner. An easier start involves climb-ing R to a roof with a crack under it. Traverse L below this to base of corner (IV+).

Routes 8 and 9 start from an easy slab found some 8m. above the water level and between the 2 great pinnacles, from either of which the slab can be reached.

8. V *   Climb to 2 facing corners. Gain base of L one with difficulty and finish up R corner and a slab wall to the R of it.

9. V   From the easy slabs move diagonally R-wards to gain a very steep corner with loose blocks at its base (almost directly above a chimney leading up to the R pinnacle ledge). Climb directly in the corner, trending R to top.

10. IV   A broken crack system directly behind the pinnacle to big tree belays.

Routes 11,12,13 and 14 start R of the big pinnacle. It is possible to traverse R to these from the pinnacle area, though the traverse is harder than any move on the climbs.

11. III *   Climb a R-trending chimney to steepening and hence a tree belay. Now easy rocks to the top.

12. V-   The tree may be reached direct by a steep crack.

13. IV+ **   A difficult traverse R from the base of no.12 leads to a small slab and possible belay. It is easier to reach this by boat. Climb a crack L-wards then direc to big ledges. Easy rock to the top.

14. IV+   From the slab of no.13, climb R-wards then straight up a crack to easy ground and the top.

15. II *   At the far R end of the crag, an obvious and deep L-facing chimney.

Gas hole on east face of Poi.

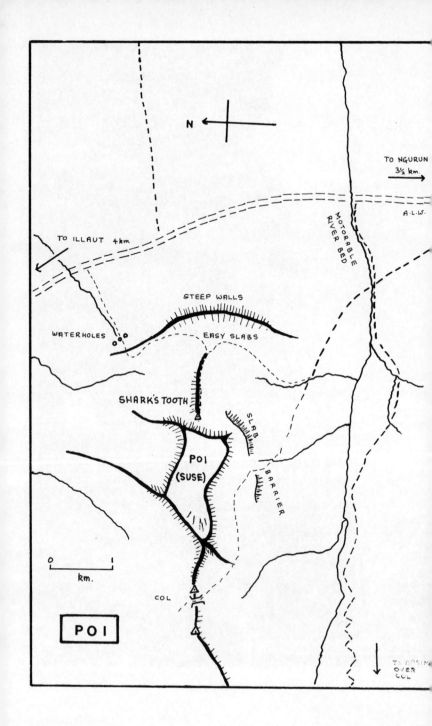

N

TO NGURUN
3½ km.

MOTORABLE RIVER BED

A.L.W.

TO ILLAUT 4km.

STEEP WALLS

WATERHOLES

EASY SLABS

SHARK'S TOOTH

SLAB

POI
(SUSE)

BARRIER

0   1
km.

COL

TO ARSIM
OVER
COL

POI

Poi

General: Poi resembles an enormous loaf of bread. At its W end a ridge leading from an obvious col provides a long, easy access route to the summit area (one short rock step is III). On all other sides the cliffs average about 500m. in height and are mainly vertical. The summit plateau is covered with grassy meadows and forest. From N to S the cliffs extend for some 3 km., and the plateau at its widest is one km. The SE (Gas Hole) face, opposite the road, is the most impressive – about 500m. high, vertical and pock marked with huge caves, some of which could accommodate a house. Vultures circle endlessly in the thermals near the cliff. The name of the face results from a misconception as to the origin of these features which are most probably caused by erosion.

The long S face has 2 major crack/chimney lines. The E one has repulsed two attempts so far by separate parties. The N side also has a promising looking line – hitherto unattempted. The climb described goes up the E-facing buttress of Poi. Several attempts were made on this by various parties before the first successful ascent, which took $3\frac{1}{2}$ days. The climb could probably now be done in 2 days, as the original problems were mainly concerned with route finding.

The nearest village is Ngurunit where a UNESCO research camp and a mission are found. Both are likely to be helpful if assistance is required and both have radio contact with the outside world. Ngurunit is located on a stream which flows out of the Ndoto Mountains. Not far below the camp it vanishes into the desert soils. Above Ngurunit it follows a beautiful, steep-sided valley. Numerous deep pools, butterflies and birds enliven walking in the shady forests. As a lot of water and equipment have to be carried up to the cliffs it is worth hiring porters at Ngurunit. Each porter will costs about 30 KSh per day. The walk to the Shark's Tooth base camp takes about half a day from Ngurunit; 1 h. can be saved by driving and leaving your vehicle by the river bed at the start of the walk-in. The porters know the best access paths to the Shark's Tooth and their local knowledge can save considerable time and energy. Good paths exist most of the way but they are difficult to follow.

From the summit descend the W ridge (one short abseil) to the col from where it is best to continue all the way down to the river bed on a reasonable path. Then either reascend to collect any kit left behind at the Shark's Tooth or make arrangements to have it brought down by porters. The traverse from the col along the base of the cliff back to the Shark's Tooth is hellish, especially in the dark. At 2000m. Poi gets quite cold at night. While climbing, the only time the cliff becomes really hot is around midday if the sun is directly on you. Water and limited mechanical assistance are obtainable at Ngurunit. The nearest garage facilities are at Maralal (180 km.).

Access: From Nairobi good tarmac roads via Naivasha, Gilgil and Nyahururu to Rumuruti (240 km.). Then a good dirt road to Maralal (125 km.), and on to Baragoi with good tea-houses (100 km.). From Baragoi the dirt road remains good until it becomes rather rocky, going over a pass leading into the South Horr Valley; beyond the pass the road is rough and a vehicle with good ground clearance is needed; one or two sandy sections may need 4 WD or planks. After a short distance in the valley a turn-off to the R (36 km. from Baragoi) leads in about 50 km. to Illaut. Ngurunit another 13 km; this last section is dominated by Poi.

An alternative approach from Nairobi is via Naro Moru to Isiolo where the tarmac ends; last petrol stations and garage facilities. Then a good dirt road to Laisamis. One km. after this a turn-off L leads to Ngurunit, some 70 km. from Laisamis; half-way along this stretch, the wide and hopefully dry Milgis riverbed is crossed. Soon after this, a turn-off R to Korr is to be avoided. This alternative is faster and the roads are slightly better, but you may be required to wait for a convoy to travel between Laisamis and Isiolo for security reasons; sometimes there is only one convoy a day. Matatus and buses do not serve the Poi area.

113 East Face of Poi   VI+   650m. ***

A.Wielochowski, R.Corkhill, 1983. $3\frac{1}{2}$ km. from Ngurunit follow a dry river bed upstream for one km. Take a path leading NW then N over giant slabs to gain a long ridge coming down from foot of the E face. Follow ridge till the Shark'sTooth blocks the way; good campsite just before this. The foot of the climb is 50m. beyond the tooth where the ridge crest meets the cliff face.

Traverse R to ledge with loose blocks at R end of overhangs. Pull onto slab above bulge, move L to grass and go up this to tree. Now L to climb a slab, then L to gain ledges; belay on L below corner by small trees (V, 35m.). A corner L of the bushes then step R via big flake into main corner. Climb this to ledges and belay (VI-, 25m.). Climb tapering rotten slab to L, then fine corner above to big ledge below overhanging walls (V+, 30m.). Gain a rotten chimney, step L to arête and take a crack just L of arête (8 aid points). Move R across a slab to easier ground and good belays 3m. higher (V+, A1, 25m.). Attain easier angled slab R of belay, and take this to slabby ledge system. Descend this R till an easy depression leads up to a grassy ledge on R (IV, 40m.). Climb slab above belay, then trend L, pas-sing some excellent runners. A further awkward movement L leads to small grassy ledge with good belays; this point is 45m. directly above belay at top of A1 pitch (IV+, 40m.). Climb diagonally upwards and L, then straight up to grassy slopes and a wide vegetated terrace. Belay on L, below a clean R-facing corner; a short way R is a shallow cave hidden behind some bushes providing a good biv. site (IV+, 50m.). Climb corner for 10m., make a long traverse L across narrow grassy ledge, then climb easier slabs trending slightly L to a very obvious tree in a niche (IV+, 55m.). Possible to belay several m. lower than the niche (pegs), so breaking this long pitch and reducing rope problems. Traverse R along very narrow ledge band till a wide broken groove is reached. Climb this, moving L at a steepening, till a L-trending, slightly vegetated ramp is reached. Follow this to a high belay place-ment 5m. short of a point directly above the previous belay (V-, 40m.). Continue along ramp to a ledge with tree belays; Arboretum Ledge, open biv. site (IV+, 40m.). Move L easily to a steep slab overlooking the overhanging Gas Hole face. Climb slab on good rock, aiming for the L of 2 chimney lines, clearly visible below a "gas hole" from the walk-in; a very serious pitch, no runners before the chimney base; belay 8m. higher, on a ledge to L (pegs, VI-, 45m.). Climb chimney and exit L. Move R to thin wall, then back L through vegetation to belay below corner (V, 30m.). Climb corner for 8m., then R and up across ledges and easy bulges to gain centre of the Gas Hole; good biv. (IV, 30m.). Move L across exposed slab to reach R-hand end of long ledge system. Climb a short wall above (VI+) and move R to vegetated corner; climb this then move L to vegetated bay and excellent belays in a horizontal slot on L; a serious pitch; the major difficulties are totally unprotected; a bolt may be justified to protect the crux (VI+, 25m.). Now step L across wall to reach slab. Climb this trending R, then vegetation to steep blank wall above and runners. Move L till pleasant slabs can be climbed trending a bit R to belay a few m. below a line of bulges and slight overhangs (V-, 40m.).

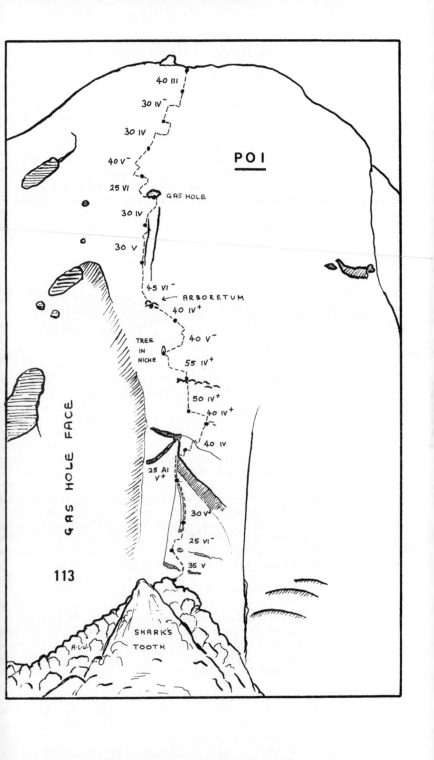

Climb through contorted break in bulge above (good runner) to vegetated ledges taken R to a slab; climb this for 2m. then go L to tree (IV, 30m.). A slab, then L on vegetated ledge, and up to tree (IV-, 30m.). Now L then easy slabs to the top (III, 40m.).

The summit is followed W till grassy slabs lead to a col; continue up the other side then abseil down a ridge step. A long traverse to the R avoids the next step. Traverse back L and so reach the main col. A path, indistinct and badly overgrown in places, runs down from col in a NE direction to the river (6 h.). It is also possible to regain the Shark's Tooth biv. from the main col by a long traverse keeping close to the cliffs; see comments under general remarks.

There is no water on Poi, which must be carried in. Also take a wide selection of chocks and wires, a medium Friend and a small variety of pegs including long blades.

○ ○ ○ ○ ○

Longido

General: Longido lies just L of the main Nairobi – Arusha road, 25 km. S of the Namanga border post. It is a steep-sided hill, about 2600m. high, with bush on its lower slopes and forest higher up. There are 2 summits; the higher E top is heavily forested on all sides. The western has numerous crags; the biggest of these is almost 300m. high and faces the main road. Although Longido is in Tanzania the problems in getting there are slight. No special currency arrangements need be made and the border crossing is relatively straightforward. So far little climbing has been done on the cliffs and there appears to be potential for some fairly hard long climbs.

Access: 25 km. S of Namanga the W face of Longido dominates the road. A radio station and reflector on the ridge above mark the access route to the central and S sections. A steep tarmac road leads from the main road up to the radio station in 2 km. There is a watchman here. Above this a clear rough path ascends to the reflector. 100m. below this traverse L and cross a stream bed to gain a ridge which soon gives easy access through shady forest to foot of the face. Crossing 2 further streams leads to a similar ridge rising to centre of the cliff. For the N end it is best to walk up game and cattle trails starting NW of the hill. The walk up on any side takes about 4 h. Bivouacs below the cliffs are plentiful and pleasant, but there is no guarantee of water though a few seasonal streams do exist in the forest belt.

It is possible to leave vehicles at the radio station. Garage facilities available in Namanga on the Kenyan side. Taking a vehicle across the border can be difficult and a Tanzanian road tax of 1000 TSh must be paid (valid for 3 months). It is just as easy to leave a vehicle at Namanga and continue by matatu to Longido.

The main W-facing cliff is cut by a prominent L to R diagonal fault. R.114 follows the most prominent chimney line in centre of the R-hand half of this cliff. The upper section quits the main chimney line and traverses R below huge roofs to find a spectacular escape to the summit ridge.

114   The Great Escape   VI-   335m. *

A.Wielochowski, R.Corkhill, 1984. Start on a big vegetated terrace just R of the chimney base.

Climb vegetated chimney to highest tree, below a steepening (45m.). Now the R side of chimney over several overlaps (crux, one aid point used on 1st overlap); belay on chockstone a few m. up the narrower part of chimney (30m.). Continue more easily deep inside chimney to good tree belay below a steepening (40m.). The chimney, then move R to gain a corner and hence a slab (one aid point used on 1st ascent). The slab to easier ground on R and a big airy ledge (35m.). The difficult wall immediately behind, then through blocks to ledge on R. Above R-hand end of ledge a crack leads up and R; climb this, then a slab above to thickly vegetated ledges (45m.). Move down and across slab on R, then up more easily to gain a long easy ramp below red overhanging walls to a tiny cave belay (35m.). Pull over cave roof, with or without aid, through bush to ledge (5m.). Traverse R to big open ledge (10m.); continue R below huge roofs; using a sling on a tree, tension down to a continuation of the traverse; after a few steep slab moves an easy traverse leads to tree belay below a chimney (35m.). Climb chimney and step R below chockstone to a ledge. Traverse R across a slab to a hidden ledge (35m.). Now go up easily to the top (20m.).
Descent: Follow ridge S till easy forest paths can be taken down or back to a biv. site.

115   West Diagonal   V+   600m. *

I.J.Allan, M.Savage, 1973. The first route to tackle the main cliff. Initially it follows the prominent fault cutting cliff from bottom L to top R. The upper half takes a chimney and gullies to the summit. The fault itself is an immense system of vegetated gullies; it has been climbed in its entirety (V). The first 150m. of R.115 uses easy slabs R of the main fault till a horizontal ledge system is reached; above this is a steepening wall. Descend and cross (V) to L side of gully. Now a crack is followed on the extreme L of gully till a ledge is reached (biv. site on 1st ascent). A slab R of the crack is climbed till a traverse L rejoins the crack. Fine chimney climbing follows for 100m. until further progress looks uninviting. Make an exposed traverse R across buttress on the R to enter a small gully and follow this to summit; there are 2 crux pitches (V) in this section; on the 1st ascent some aid was used on both.

Other areas

Many other crags in Kenya offer climbing routes. More are totally unexplored. A few of the former are described briefly below and the reader is left to find routes for himself.

TAITA HILLS

Follow the road from Voi to Taveta. After several km. a tarmac road leads R up to

Wundanyi in these hills. Several large unexplored cliffs in this area. A big cliff above Yale (very near Wundanyi) has been climbed; the rock here is featureless and lichenous.

LOITA HILLS

Several cliffs are found in this area. Most of them are very remote. One has been explored... the Lost Aloe Cliff. From Narok take road to the Masai Mara. Turn L towards Morijo and follow this road to village of Naro Osura. The road then climbs spectacularly into the hills. 2.7km. from highest point on the road, a valley on the R leads to crag, about one km. from the main road. The climbing is steep and quite good. Walking and camping in this area are superb.

NAIBOR ENKEJU

Driving from Rumuruti to Maralal a major road leads off R to Wamba. This is 19 km. from Maralal. Continue towards Maralal for about 5 km. and turn R at a small village (Kisima). In about 4 km. the S end of a hill is reached. The E face is a very fine 150m. cliff. Climbs can be reached in 10 min. from a car. The cliff has been thoroughly explored by Robert Chambers and others. Detailed route descriptions and diagrams are given in MCK Bulletin No. 58. Among the variety of fine climbs here, the best area is R of centre. Please obtain permission to climb from the Chief at Kisima.

The areas below are all located near Isiolo. They were mainly explored and developed by Ian Howell who has written a short guide to the zone in MCK Bulletin, 68.

NATORBE

Follow road from Isiolo to Archer's Post for approx. 40 km. About 2 km. S of the bridge before Archer's Post, turn R down a track, leading to the Shaba National Reserve. In 3 km. Natorbe hill, just S of the Ewaso Ngiro River, is reached. Park just before the entrance gate to the Reserve. The 80m. high cliffs are hidden on the E side. The rock is good and is reached in about 20 min. walk from the gate. Facing E, the afternoon provides the coolest period. A variety of routes have been done. Excellent game viewing into the adjoining protected area from the climbs.

OLOLOKWE

Driving 16 km. N from Archer's Post this cliff is clearly visible. It is one of Kenya's biggest cliffs; 2 km. long and over 400m. high. At present there are few climbs on it. Those done follow the only major weaknesses and are vegetated. Vast areas of smooth featureless rock exist and there is more scope for some fine, hard routes. Further R the summit of some smaller cliffs just below a radio station can be reached by a steep motorable track. These offer some worthwhile shorter routes. Abseil down in 2 long stages.

CAT AND MOUSE

Just past Ololokwe, on R side of the road, are 2 pinnacles. The top of the Mouse is reached by a pleasant aid climb (bolts in place). The Cat can be scaled more easily.

The Kiondo hut in the Ruwenzori.

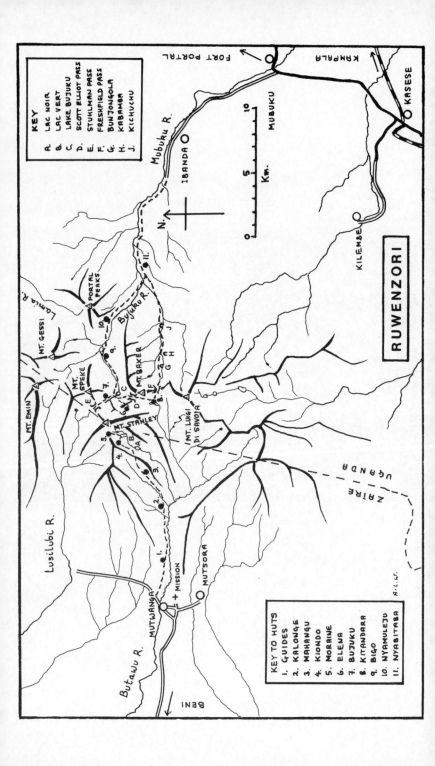

RUWENZORI

KEY

- A. LAC NOIR
- B. LAC VERT
- C. LAKE BUJUKU
- D. SCOTT ELLIOT PASS
- E. STUHLMAN PASS
- F. FRESHFIELD PASS
- G. BUNJONGOLA
- H. KABARASA
- J. KICHUCHU

KEY TO HUTS

1. GUIDES
2. KALONGE
3. MAHANGU
4. KIONDO
5. MORAINE
6. ELENA
7. BUJUKU
8. KITANDARA
9. BIGO
10. NYAMULEJU
11. NYABITABA

Km.
0   5   10

N.

FORT PORTAL
KAMPALA
KASESE
MUBUKU
IBANDA
Mubuku R.
KILEMBE
Byjuku R.
PORTAL PEAKS
MT. GESSI
Lusilubi R.
MT. EMIN
MT. SPEKE
MT. STANLEY
MT BAKER
MT. LUIGI DI SAVOIA
UGANDA
ZAIRE
Butawu R.
MUTWANGA
+ MISSION
MUTSORA
BENI

A.L.W.

RUWENZORI

GENERAL

THE Ruwenzori (The Mountains of the Moon) form the westernmost boundary of East Africa and differ considerably from the isolated volcanic peaks of Mt. Kenya and Kilimanjaro. They represent a true mountain chain composed of several major massifs. The highest, the Stanley Group (Margherita, 5109m.), is the third highest peak in Africa, and the Stanley Plateau is the largest glaciated area. Also outstanding are picturesque lakes and lush vegetation. For visitors from Europe access to the area is often normally best via Nairobi. The range is renowned for bad weather. There are distinct dry seasons and the climate on the W side is drier than the E. Lingering mist is a frequent problem and makes route finding difficult.

Walking in the Ruwenzori is very demanding; only those equipped for and accustomed to tough trekking and trail-breaking should go there. The central areas are remote from help and medical facilities; accidents must be avoided and parties should carry adequate medical supplies. On the Uganda side the best approach is from Ibanda village, where for many years now John Matte has organised porter services. These men belong to the Bakonjo tribe, a tough, friendly and co-operative people. Guides generally speak good Swahili and reasonable English. Hire rates in Uganda are likely to be greatly changed by recent political and economic upheavals. The usual charges are therefore not quoted; these are applied to guides, porters and food per day; to blanket and clothing rent for porters per trek/expedition. Black market rates for hard currency exchange are common; in 1984/85 one US dollar = at least USh 550.

Poor accommodation can be found at Ibanda. Various huts on the mountain trails are mostly run down and rock shelters are often a better proposition. The Uganda side is not a national park and no hut charges are levied. Many parties have been rather careless over litter and sanitary arrangements, and certain huts are quite unpleasant. Vegetation in the bogs has also suffered and paths have been churned into sometimes knee-deep mud.

On both the Uganda and Zaire slopes the best period is late December to February, though June to early August can be quite good. Other months are unsuitable; during heavy rains rivers in the deep valleys become swollen and difficult to cross while the paths are extremely boggy.

The Zaire side is part of the Virunga National Park. Park offices at Mutsora offer poor accommodation or better camping. Fees are paid on entry and the park organizes porters and guides. Fees in 1984:

Park entry charge, Za.600. Hut fees (per person per night), 45. Camera, 50. Porter food (per man per day), 45. Porter wage (per day), 50. Camping charge (per tent per night), 45. 1985 exchange rate: US $ = 40 Zaire. Black market and official rates are similar. Legal currency exchange is almost impossible and street trading is normally accepted.

The park provides a free guide. Porters are not obliged to carry more than 18 kg, and may be reluctant to carry past Kiondo Hut if snow lies on the ground; the local people are very friendly and porters provide an excellent service; they speak Swahili and often fluent French. The exact role of a guide, some of whom speak good English, is not clearly defined. Huts on the access trail were built during the Belgian colonial period. The first 3 are solidly constructed and while virtually no maintenance has

133

been done on them in the last 20 years they still provide acceptable accommodation.

The Zaire approach follows a steep and fairly dry ridge giving strenuous walking. The hotel at Mutwanga is at present being rebuilt by Patrick Ingels. While there are a few small shops here, suitable provisioning is difficult and food should be brought in. This applies to the Ugandan side as well.

ACCESS

Uganda Recent internal problems still prohibit firm recommendations. In normal circumstances petrol is available. From Nairobi, rail service to Kampala; also a cheap bus and matatu. Overnight train Kampala - Kasese (4.30pm-7.00am) leaving on Monday, Wednesday, Friday. From Kasese, taxi hire to Ibanda (30 min.), costs at least USh 5500.

Zaire International flights to Kigali. From here, rough roads via Goma and Beni to Mutwanga. Vehicle hire in Kigali or Goma; cheap lorry rides possible. Alternatively (see comments above), fly to Entebbe (Uganda) and take the Kampala-Kasese train; then by public transport, lorries etc. drive round S end of the range. The most expensive but expedient plan is by charter aircraft from Wilson airport in Nairobi to Mutwanga, which has an all-weather airstrip one km. long, located 8 km. W of the village. The journey from western Zaire (Kinshasa) to the Ruwenzori is very long and tedious. Note that hiring vehicles anywhere is expensive.

WALKING ROUTES

Ugandan approach via Bujuku.

Day 1. From road end at Nykalengij (1600m.), 5 km. past Ibanda, follow a path on the L, crossing stream after 400m., and continue through elephant grass then bush. After $1\frac{1}{4}$ h. it leaves the river and climbs steeply on the S side into forest then drops slightly to cross 2 more streams. In 30 min. it crosses a small river then climbs a steep ridge to reach the Nyabitaba hut (2620m.) and a rock shelter nearby ($4\frac{1}{2}$ h. from roadhead). Poor hut with rough floor space for 12 people; tent spaces nearby.
Day 2. A path along ridge for about 500m. then take a R fork descending steeply through bamboo to the Mubuku River, just below its confluence with the Bujuku. If logs are not in place it may be necessary to wade the river. Follow path now on N side of the Bujuku to a good rockshelter, Kanyasabu (2 h.). Continue ahead to the Nyamuleju Hut (3300m.); collapsed floor, 6 places, no tent spaces ($2\frac{1}{2}$ h.). It is better to continue to Bigo.
Day 3. After Nyamuleju the path follows N bank of the Bujuku through more open scenery in the giant heather and groundsel zone. Cross the Bujuku at lower end of Bigo Bog. Just above this lies the Bigo Hut (3400m.) and a rockshelter; pleasant hut with room for 10 ($2\frac{1}{2}$ h.). The next section is unpleasant and muddy, following S side of the Bujuku to cross stream just before the Bujuku Lake ($2\frac{1}{2}$ h.), then along its NE shore to the Cooking Pot Cave and Bujuku Huts, 3993m. (30 min.); room for 9 in one hut, the other is used by porters; pleasant campsites. Descent from here to roadhead, about 9 h. Beyond huts path continues to the Stuhlmann Pass.
Day 4. Cross swampy streams beyond the Cooking Pot Cave and go S up Groundsel Gully to a level platform (40 min.). The path divides (L for Scott Elliot Pass); follow R fork, passing a rockshelter after 10 min., then steeply in a WSW direction to ridge crest at 4480m. (2 h. from swamps). Now a cairned line W winds among slabs and low walls to the Elena Huts, 4541m. (30 min. from ridge crest). One hut in good condition sleeps 4, the other is collapsed. Restricted tentspace; no

vegetation hereabouts. Descent to Bujuku, 1½ h.

Ugandan approach via Kitandara.

Day 1. As for the Bujuku approach.

Day 2. The ridge path for 500m. to a fork R (to Bujuku, ignore). Follow ridge ahead and 1 h. after leaving hut traverse R, dropping gently to the Mubuku river. Cross improvised bridge 100m. upstream or wade river. On N side of the river go through bamboo and swamp to a poor rockshelter, Kuchuku (2 h. from river). Above this ascend to cliff top and follow path W along the Mubuku to a nice open location on S side of stream, Kabamba rockshelter, 3600m. (6 h. from Nyabitaba; 4 h. in descent).

Day 3. In 1 h. another fine sheltered area, Bujongolo, is reached, where the path continues W in open ground to Freshfield Pass (4360m.), 4 h. from Kabamba. After a short traverse NW, it drops steeply to Kitandara lakes and hut (3990m.) in 1 h. Allow 4 h. in reverse. The hut, in good condition, is beautifully located on the shore of the lower lake; room for 16.

Day 4. The muddy path along E side of valley through groundsel forest for 40 min. to a drier and more open part, passing a pond below the W face of Mt. Baker. A boulder maze leads to the Scott Elliot Pass (4372m.) in 2 h. A descent N takes you to Bujuku. For the Elena huts descend slightly on the other side, to double back SW before the path drops steeply. Well cairned, it soon turns NW to attain ridge crest described in the Bujuku approach (30 min. from pass). 2 h. in reverse.

Zaire approach.

Day 1. From Mutsora (1200m.) a 40 min. walk to Mutwanga commercial centre, passing a run-down hospital. (A Belgian priest runs a mission found a short way up-hill from the hospital; the former Mutwanga hotel stands one km. above Mutwanga). From the shops continue N, cross the Butawu stream and shortly turn R to take a path gently uphill, leading in 2 h. to the Guides Hut (Kiandolire, 1700m.) beside the forest. Sleeping room for 10, also fresh water on request. Now through fine forest for 3 h. with stepping stones over 2 major streams, the 2nd. one providing a water supply for the Kalonge Hut (2140m.) 10 min. away; room for 16; tent spaces.

Day 2. A path N from hut soon swings E and drops steeply to a stream crossing; last water. Then it climbs a steep ridge to a resting spot (Hotel des Assetre, 2440m.), 1½ h. Here offerings are left to the mountain gods. In a further 1½ h. reach a fine knoll (2910m.); now the trek becomes tougher as the path mounts steeply through tangles of giant heather and deep mosses for 2 h. more to Mahangu hut (3310m.); room for 16; tent spaces. A tiny "well" lies just E of the hut; if this is dry porters fetch from a distant stream.

Day 3. The path continues steeply in tangled heather roots, beautiful but strenuous. A stream (3740m.) is reached in 2 h. Now easier ground for 1 h. to Kampi ya Chupa (4030m.), a flat ridge top and fine viewpoint attained by Stuhlmann in 1891. Lastly, along an open ridge with superb views of Lac Noir, to the Kiondo hut (4300m.), 1 h. Room for 12, tent spaces, stream 5 min. N of hut. Porters hut located lower down by stream. 40 min. NE of hut, Wasuwamesu summit (4462m.) affords a magnificent view of the Stanley Group.

Day 4. At a small col just E of hut a path goes down to a short step with fixed cable, then steeply down a muddy, slabby gully to traverse along to the Lac Vert (4160m.). From its N end the path rises steeply to Lac Gris; fine campsite at the point where path levels out. So reach in another 45 min. Moraine (Glacier) hut (4495m.), at upper vegetation limit, 3 h. from Kiondo. Hut leaks in bad weather,

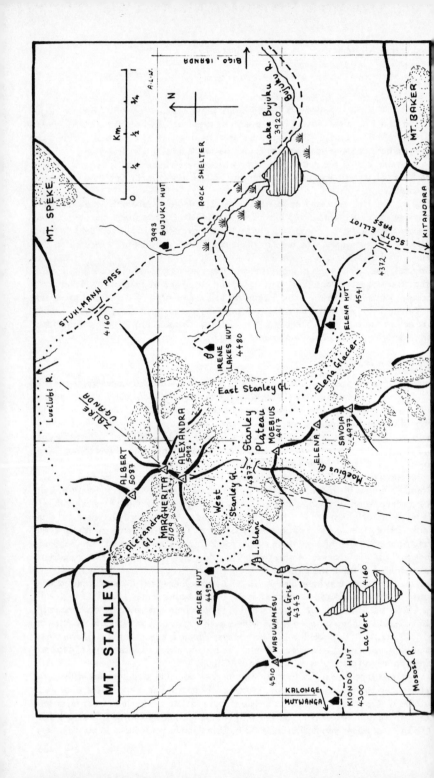

room for 4; one tent space nearby. This approach can be reversed in 2 days.

The fastest route from Moraine Hut to the Ugandan side entails crossing the Stanley Plateau. Going round Albert to the Stuhlmann Pass involves problematic route finding and some scrambling. A traverse SW to Kitandara takes 12 h. of laborious walking through vegetation and over mossy slabs.

CLIMBS

116 Stanley Plateau (from Elena Huts)   1 *   1½ h.

The Duke of Abruzzi, J.Petigax, C.Ollier, J.Brocherel, 1906. Normal route to the Plateau; fine views and simple access to the Stanley Group summits; crampons useful. Just above the huts reach the Elena gl. and ascend near its centre, avoiding crevasses as necessary. In descent, from centre of the Plateau just below Moebius, compass bearing 310° (45 min.).

117 Alexandra SE Ridge   1/2 ***   1½ h.

First ascent as R.116. From Plateau follow ridge to summit, turning obstacles L. Most of the climb is on snow/ice with a few rocky sections near the top. Continuation to Margherita across the Margherita-Alexandra col takes 1½ h. (grade 1) if a way can be found avoiding crevasses.

118 Margherita E Ridge   1/2 **   3 h.

G.N.Humphreys, E.H.Armitage, R.T.Wickham, G.Oliver, 1926. From the ridge of R.117 find a way on to gl. between this ridge and Margherita; reach the E ridge of latter and follow to summit. (A better way is to gain the Margherita-Alexandra col, and ascend directly from there). From Margherita a short scramble down easy rocks leads to a snowy ridge and the top of Albert, grade 1 (15 min.).

119 Stanley Plateau (from W)   1/2 *   2-3 h. from Moraine Hut.

J.J.David, 1904. Route depends on snow cover. Originally the gl. was mounted from a point due E of Lac Blanc; keeping to its S side, the NW foot of Moebius is reached; often steep and icy. With good snow it may be better to follow gullies then snowslopes keeping to N side of the gl. When the angle eases a long rising traverse R leads to the Plateau.

120 Margherita W Face   1/2 **   3-4 h.

K. de Grunne, W.J.Ganshof van der Meersch, P.Solvay, J.Georges, H. de Schryver, 1932. Various ways. Above the moraine of Moraine Hut, in dry conditions easy rocks can be climbed direct to avoid the lower ice-fall on your R. In good snow conditions it is easier to climb the gl. throughout; for this start 50m. E of Hut, descend slightly and traverse to base of gl. Avoid ice and rock cliffs by working L, then climb gl., keeping generally near the centre. A long snow pitch is possible in the lower part, then a crevassed section. In the upper half a steep rock outcrop is turned L or R to gain the Margherita-Alexandra col. From here easier terrain to summit. The gl. is suitable for descent in good snow conditions.

121 Albert NW Ridge   IV- (rock) ***   3-4 h.

K. de Grunne, J. de la Vallée-Poussin, W.J.Ganshof, J.Georges, 1932. Reach the base of Alexandra gl. Make a rising traverse over gl. to the lower of the two prominent shoulders on ridge (this is part of the traverse towards the Stuhlmann Pass). Now climb ridge; avoid a vertical step by a 30m. traverse L, then easy rocks on L side to the higher shoulder. Above this another vertical step is turned by a 50m. traverse R, returning to crest over steep rocks, then easy rocks to the summit.

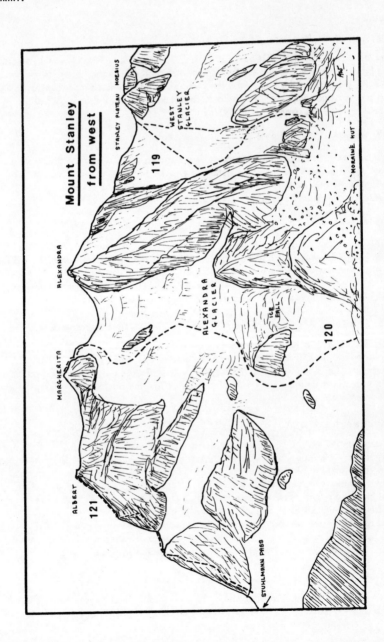

Part of Leviathan cave system.

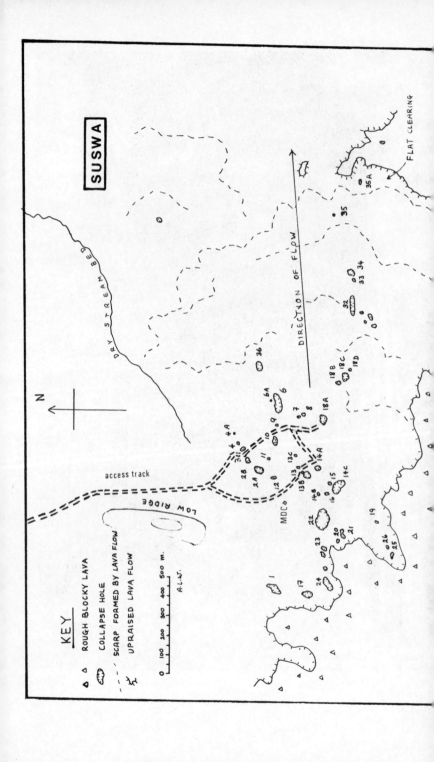

CAVES

INTRODUCTION

Two readily accessible and fascinating caving areas in Kenya are recommended for special consideration. They comprise of lava tubes systems, formed in a period of recent volcanic activity, and are totally different from limestone caves. Relatively rare, they are believed to have been formed when molten lava, of the correct type and viscosity, flowed down a slope of an ideal angle. The outer layers cool and solidify, but the core continues to flow and in some cases evacuates itself completely to leave behind an empty tube. Numerous unusual features can be found and include lava ropes, benches, lava stalactites and stalagmites and a variety of secondary formations. The latter are produced by the deposition of minerals dissolved in the ground waters. The secondary formations are exceptionally fine in cave 35A on Suswa where very unusual and beautiful stalactites and stalagmites are found. Many of these formations are extremely fragile and great care must be taken not to touch them. Primary lava tube formations are a record of the past and any damage done to them will never heal.

Suswa is a magnificent example of an extinct volcano in the Rift Valley. Many caves are found on its E slopes. None of them are long or complex and no special equipment or knowledge are required to tackle the system. Leviathan is located in the Chyulu Hills and is at present the world's second longest lava tube system. The total length of its passages add up to over 11 km. The complete traverse is possible in one long hard day. This would be quite demanding as long sections of the tube involve balancing over slippery boulders. There are also a few short squeezes. Near the top of Leviathan a short length of rope would be useful to help negotiate traverses on the poor, steep rock in this section.

Numerous animals inhabit the caves and some others have fallen into them. There are several skeletons of large animals in Leviathan; none of these should be touched. Several different varieties of bats inhabit the caves. Their guano can be unpleasant and slippery to walk through. The bats themselves pose no real hazard; as they are not carnivorous they are not rabid.

The entrances to the caves are invariably formed by Collapse Holes where the roof of the tube has fallen in. The vegetation around these holes is dense and often includes a characteristic palm-like tree (Dracaena), or a fig tree. On Suswa collapse holes are best located by orienteering techniques (10m. = about 12 paces).

SUSWA

Access: Take the old road from Nairobi to Naivasha (the more westerly). After 58 km, just before reaching Longonot, turn L onto a good tarmac road leading to Narok. After 10 km. a satellite station is passed on the L; in another $6\frac{1}{2}$ km. along this road a dirt road leads S towards Suswa. Now go 6km. across plains to a Masai manyatta. Just beyond this a track leads SSW up the slopes of Suswa; it is very rough and fairly steep but a well driven saloon car will get up it. In 5 km. the edge of the caldera is reached at a meadow. Immediately take a fork L and head S for 3 km. (ignore a R at $2\frac{1}{2}$ km.) to a big collapse hole, 18A, surrounded by shady fig trees at approx. grid ref. 113748 on sheet 147/2 Ol Doinyo Onyoke (in 1/50,000 national grid pattern for Kenya, DOS type 423, Series Y731). This offers a good

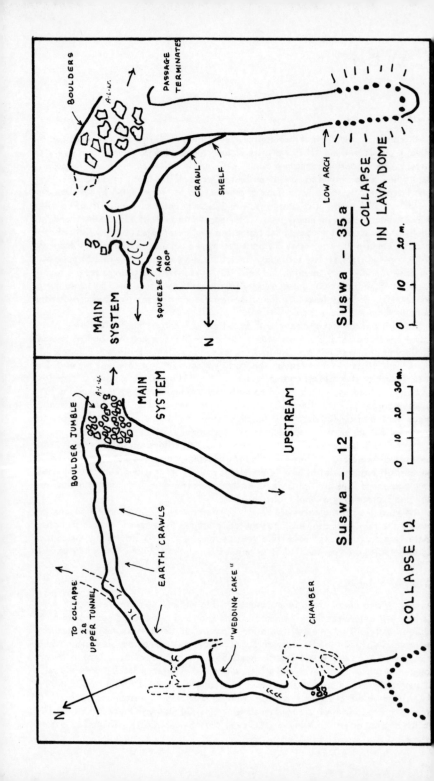

Suswa – 35a

COLLAPSE IN LAVA DOME

BOULDERS

A.L.W.

PASSAGE TERMINATES

CRAWL

SHELF

LOW ARCH

MAIN SYSTEM

SQUEEZE AND DROP

N

0   10   20 m.

Suswa – 12

BOULDER TUMBLE

A.L.W.

MAIN SYSTEM

UPSTREAM

EARTH CRAWLS

TO COLLAPSE 28 UPPER TUNNEL

"WEDDING CAKE"

CHAMBER

N

0   10   20   30 m.

COLLAPSE 12

campsite but no water. Just before 18A the track skirts R of the small entrance to collapse 9.

The R fork from the meadow leads in 9 km. to a good viewpoint overlooking the Moat and Raft of the volcano; from here a pleasant half day walk leads to the summit and back.

Public transport is available as far as the manyatta at the base of Suswa. Garage facilities at the Narok turn-off on the Nairobi to Naivasha road.

Caves

18A. Grade I. This is the longest cave system. Several collapse holes lead into it. At the upflow end a lower tube can be reached with the help of an in-situ ladder.

6. Grade I. Another long system, with several collapses leading into it. At the lower end there are some interesting, steep passages and side tubes to be explored.

6A. Grade II. A very interesting cave. The entrance is a tiny hole, located in a small clump of bushes, about 40m. N of 6 and not far from its E end. Gaining entry is the crux.

12. Grade II-. Probably the most interesting cave system of its size in Kenya. It links up with hole 2B. Three earthy crawls lead into a deeper big tunnel; downflow climb to higher level and a short crawl L leads to the most beautiful sections.

MDC. Moby Dick Cave. Tiny hole below bush, 255° and 80m. from entrance to cave 12. A short way in, an earthy drop leads to a narrow resonating tube. Further in other passages are also worthy of a visit.

35A. Grade I+. This cave is located in a large flat clearing, below a rocky vegetated scarp. An elevated lava-flow blocks the clearing to the E. Entry is gained via a collapsed, typically-vegetated lava dome, about 20m. long (E-W) and 10m. wide. A low arch leads E into a wider and higher passage. A shelf on the L leads into a low crawl passage. After this turn L and go down a lava step into the system proper.

LEVIATHAN

Access: Almost 200 km. from Nairobi along the Mombasa road lies the village of Kibwezi. About $1\frac{1}{2}$ km. after the petrol station, a good dirt road leads off R. Follow this SSW for $6\frac{1}{2}$ km. to where it forks R (SW). Continue SW, past some waterholes, to a village in another 6 km. The road gradually deteriorates, along to Milangi village in a further $3\frac{1}{2}$ km. Continue and pass a baptist church on the L; in one km. a track branches R to Kisula Hill; about $6\frac{1}{2}$ km. after this junction on the L(W) fork, one reaches a sharp L bend (here the track bears SE and starts a long ascent). Just before the L bend a rough track W leads to a hollow in the hillside, clearly visible from the road, with a shamba in it (Jonah's). Camping here by arrangement with Jonah who can also find a guide to take parties to the caves (Swahili: shimo). From the shamba a good path leads N through the forest then into more open, cultivated country. The easiest cave entrance to locate is Discovery, about 30 min. walk. Other residents in the vicinity will gladly shepherd parties back for a small reward - should you exit at a more remote collapse.

If the R fork after Milangi is taken, a very rough track leads past Kisula Hill to the central sections of Leviathan. At the following distances from the fork R from

143

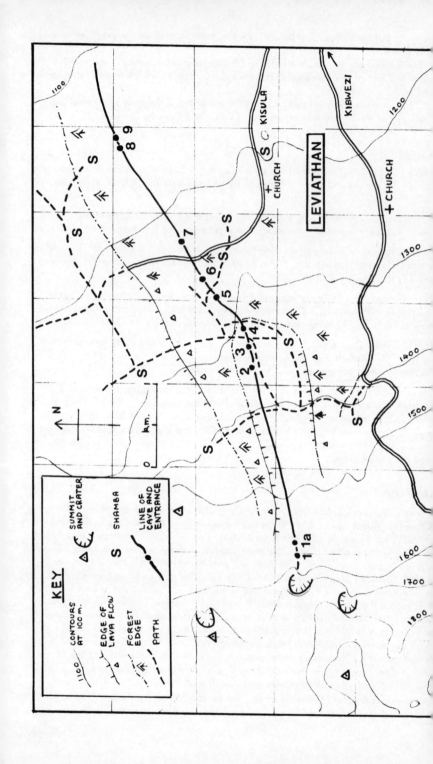

KEY

1100	CONTOURS AT 100 m.
	EDGE OF LAVA FLOW
	FOREST EDGE
	PATH
△	SUMMIT AND CRATER
S	SHAMBA
	LINE OF CAVE AND ENTRANCE

N

km.

0

LEVIATHAN

KISULA
CHURCH
CHURCH
KIBWEZI

1100
1200
1300
1400
1500
1600
1700
1800

the main track note: at 1.8km. ignore a fork R; at 2.8km. ignore a fork R and shortly another L; at 3.2km. ignore a fork R; at 4.5km. pass just R of Kisula Hill; at 4.9km. pass a small shop on L; at 5.5km. the track flattens out at 1240m. On the R nearby is the shamba of Julius Chyule (PO Box 57, Masongaleni, Kibwezi). He will act as a guide to the cave entrances and organize camping, etc. The easiest entrance to find is Forest Collapse.

There is no water in the cave area and one of the main hardships for the local people is the carrying of water. Garage facilities are at Kibwezi. Public transport cannot be relied upon for the last 12 km. to the caves. There is fine walking on the Chyulu Hills not far above Ash Cone collapse. Also, plenty of scope for further exploration on the eastern slopes of the Chyulus and maybe more Leviathans could be found.

Caves

This is a uniaxial system. Over long sections there are two or more levels. The lowest tube is most frequently followed. Technically the cave is straightforward, especially below Ash Cone collapse. However it is a serious undertaking because rescue from most sections of the cave would take a long time to mount and would be extremely difficult to execute. It is due to the efforts of the Cave Exploration Group of East Africa, and in particular to Jim Simons, that the caves were discovered and explored so thoroughly. Group members are best contacted through the Museum Society in Nairobi.

The general notes below on cave entrances/collapses are qualified with UIAA rock gradings. Grid references (GR) for their location are approximate and taken from map sheet no. 182/2 Chyulu (1/50,000 national grid pattern for Kenya in DOS type 423, Series Y731).

1. <u>Ash Cone</u> GR 699198. At base of a ridge forming the N arm of a "corrie". 300m. up the slope a short wooded gully points towards the small wooded collapse area at the top end of a large meadow. To gain upper level, take a crawl upflow. To gain lower level, go 30m. up tunnel, climb down 2 levels (loose rock, II), or make an exposed traverse (II) on L wall and continue upstream.

1a. <u>Hyena</u> Crawl in to upper level, or abseil to lower level.

2. <u>Discovery</u> GR 721202. Semi-clear area; path passes close by and tall trees surround the collapse. This is the best known entry by people living in Jonah's area. Walk in to upper level. To reach lower level, make a short traverse (I), then scramble down easily.

3 & 4. <u>Bushbuck</u> and <u>Bivvy</u>. GR 723203 and 726204. Both are in semi-clear country, near to paths. Bushbuck has a walk-in to upper level; abseil into the lower (V- to climb out). For the upper level of Bivvy, climb down a tree, or swing down over bulges to ledges (IV); walk in to lower level.

5. <u>Forest</u> GR 730207. Located in a clearing in the forest, again characterised by tall trees. Follow the main path down from Discovery over 2 lava steps for about 15 min. Also easily reached from Julius' shamba in 15 min. The upper and lower levels are walk-ins downflow; the lower level upflow involves a difficult to locate squeeze. Note: some 40m. from Forest Collapse, on a bearing of 280°, lies a tiny collapse hole (ABC) with a small system leading off up and down stream.

6 & 7. <u>Compass</u> and <u>K.M.</u> GR 732209 and 737211. These are both in the forest and can be difficult to locate from above. Compass upper level is an easy

drop; the lower is a walk in downflow and squeeze in upflow. K.M. upper level is an easy drop; the lower involves an exposed traverse in on ledges R (IV), facing downflow.

8 & 9. Reconnaissance and Pottery   GR 747219 and 748219.   Both these are in the forest. The upper collapse is not too far from a shamba. To reach the shamba walk 200m. N from the collapse. Ask here for directions to return to Jonah's or Julius' area. The shamba and cave would be difficult to locate from the outside world. Both entrances have a walk in to upper level, and a squeeze in upflow to reach lower level.

Notes on passages

Ash Cone to top of flow   30 min.
Lower passage leads easily to the end. Gaining the lower passage from Ash Cone Collapse needs about 15m. of rope; this is used to make a difficult traverse along the L wall. The top passage is followed, passing an exposed drop to its R. The lower passage is reached by climbing down a short drop on the L.   Var: instead of the difficult traverse, climbing down a hole (easy, but loose) enters a middle passage level, then straight down (pole for assistance) into the lowest level.

Ash Cone to Discovery $2\frac{1}{2}$ h.
Tedious boulders to cross initially. Skeletons. 5m. steep down-climbing over a lava fall (I). Fine sinuous passages in the lower half.

Discovery to Bushbuck   10 min.   Bat colony.

Bushbuck to Bivvy   30 min.
20m. crawl on L, through collapse debris. Bridge out of trench (III).

Bivvy to Forest   1 h.
Mud Hall Series. Tedious "mud" covered boulders. One short wall climb on L (III) at a cirque of walls. Near end, ash crawl on R. Shortly squeeze out on L into Forest Collapse.

Forest to Compass   15 min. Easy passage and pop-up into Compass.

Compass to K.M.   30 min. Goliath. A very high passage.

K.M. to Reconnaissance and Pottery $1\frac{1}{2}$ h.
Goliath continues. Endless breakdown boulders to cross. High spectacular passages. Magnificent hanging roots just below K.M. Pop-out into Reconnaissance; Pottery is reached by a similar pop-out in a very short time.

Pottery to End   1 h.
Big easy passage. Lower towards end. Several bat colonies. Long guano crawl to end.

BANTU UTAMANDUNI LODGE

The Lodge is located 170km. north of Nairobi, on the forested lower slopes of Mt. Kenya. Comfortable accommodation, camping, wholesome food, reliable guides, porters and transport services make this an ideal base for your safaris in the Mt. Kenya region.

A **6 DAY MOUNT KENYA TREK** leaves Nairobi every Saturday and includes a walk round the peaks, a visit to the Temple in Gorges Valley, an ascent of Point Lenana and a night at the Lodge.

Also available:

* **3 day walk on Mt. Kenya**
* **Trout Fishing in the Burguret, Nanyuki and Liki Rivers**
* **Visits to the: Mau Mau Caves, Natural Salt Lick, and Mountain Forest Game Reserve**
* **Traditional Dancing at the Lodge.**

Enquiries: P.O. Box 333, Nanyuki or Tel. Burguret 1.
Bookings through:

Kenya Wildlife Trails Ltd.

P.O. Box 44687, Nairobi.
Tel: 28960 Telex: 25711 Cable: WILDTRAILS

Also TOURS and CAR HIRE

KWT is centrally located in Kimathi House opposite the New Stanley Hotel.

EXECUTIVE WILDERNESS PROGRAMMES *hire mountaineering and camping equipment and act as the mountain advisers to Bantu Lodge clients.*

Nairobi Office: P.O. Box 44827, Tel: 60728, Telex: 23244 MEHR
Head Office: 5 Stile Rd, Headington, Oxford, England.

Executive Wilderness Programmes

was formed by a team of experts to give those with specialised interests the opportunity of gaining a greater insight into the fascinating diversity of peoples, landforms, flora and fauna, to be found in East Africa.

Other than the programmes outlined below, our professional expertise and contacts can also be used to provide programmes tailored to meet particular requirements.

* OUTDOOR ACTION
For the young and fit. Walking through and camping in the more remote big game country of Kenya. Meeting Masai warriors, a taste of caving, orienteering, climbing and sailing, a special course at the Kenya Outward Bound School and an ascent of Kilimanjaro.

* STUDY COURSES
Local experts, university lecturers and professors will run lecture-seminars on a variety of East African topics. Field trips to selected areas in Kenya will complement the study sessions. Courses will be run in: Human Ecology, Wildlife Studies, Geology and Anthropology.

* MOUNTAINEERING AND WILDERNESS TRAVEL
A variety of exciting safaris take you to some of the most remote corners of East Africa: the northern deserts and Lake Turkana, Loita Hills, Great Rift Valley, the lava tube caves of Mt. Suswa and the Chyulu Hills, Tsavo National Park, Mt. Kenya, Mt. Elgon, Kilimanjaro and the Ruwenzori.

* TECHNICAL CLIMBING
Guiding and instruction are available on climbs ranging from the vertical ice of the Diamond Couloir on Mt. Kenya to beginners rock climbing at Lukenya. From a expedition up Margherita in the Ruwenzori to a grade VI route at Hell's Gate.

* SAFARI RALLY
A unique opportunity to follow the world's toughest rally by air and by 4WD vehicles. Meeting and working with a service team. A few days by the Indian Ocean and a safari to one of the game parks.

* FLYING SAFARIS
Scenic flights, air transport, logistic support, para drops and aerial surveys.

ENQUIRIES:
**EXECUTIVE WILDERNESS PROGRAMMES,
5 STILE ROAD, HEADINGTON, OXFORD,
ENGLAND.   TEL. (0865) 62340.**

KENYA CONTACT:
P.O. BOX 44827, NAIROBI.

General Index